C·O·A·S·T·A·L
Nova Scotia
Outdoor Adventure Guide

Joanne Light

NIMBUS
PUBLISHING LTD

Nimbus Publishing Limited
P.O. Box 9301, Station A
Halifax, N.S. B3K 5N5
(902) 455-4286

Design: Arthur B. Carter, Halifax
Printed and bound in Canada

The financial support of the Nova Scotia Co-operative Agreement is acknowledged.

Photo credits: Irwin Barrett pp. x, 3, 48, 59, 95 (top), 109; Phyllis Blades pp. 13, 74; Keith Vaughan pp. 22, 33, 53, 88, 104 (top), 112, 117, 120, 133, 134 (top); Scott Cunningham front cover, pp. 26, 45, 64, 70, 83, 101, 124; Nova Scotia Tourism pp. 36 (top), 55, 104 (bottom), 130, 134 (bottom); Pictou County Tourist Assoc. pp. 36 (bottom), 37; Enterprise Cape Breton Corporation pp. 61, 67; Terry James p. 95 (bottom); Wayne Barrett p. 128.

Canadian Cataloguing in Publication Data

Light, Joanne, 1952-

Coastal Nova Scotia

Includes bibliographical references.
ISBN 1-55109-043-0

1. Coasts—Nova Scotia—Recreational use—Guidebooks.
2. Outdoor recreation—Nova Scotia—Guidebooks.
3. Nova Scotia—Guidebooks. I. Title.

GV191.46.N6L53 1993   917.1604'4   C93-098542-7

Contents

Dories at North Medford.

Introduction

This book is a guide for humans, yet it is about many species. It aims to establish an awareness of the coastal world of Nova Scotia so that we may better appreciate its myriad species, the geology, climate, and the countless activities available in the natural world.

The land and sea unite to produce a wealth of life and a way of life that the people who live here treasure. The variety of animal, fish, bird, and plant life that populate Nova Scotia's shores will reveal itself to you if you take the time to travel off the highways to the quiet shores, to "Stop and smell the dulse," so to speak.

You will sense how man's own history is inextricably linked with this amazing world of nature and how our technological vision of the world has veiled our eyes to this truth.

Intricately woven into the natural fabric of these regions is the cultural and economic history of the peoples who have lived here, and made their imprint on the landscape.

In this present age we find ourselves returning to an awareness of the land and life around us. In the wake of species depletion, we begin to see what we have done and ponder what is to be done. This guide invites you to share the natural and human world that is ours.

Each chapter in this book describes specific geographical regions based on geological, climatic, soil, vegetation, and animal features. Chapters are divided into areas representing a distinctive natural region with features which are specific to it, even though it forms part of the larger, more general region.

Each chapter also describes activities offered by the natural terrain of Nova Scotia in which you can participate as you travel its long and varied coastline. Along the way, you will be introduced to unusual and exciting phenomena, from fossil finds to natural heritage areas, from succulent sea culinary delights to endangered species.

As you travel here, remember that this place belongs to many species, just one of whom is man.

Cynthia Lamson

Acknowledgements

Several people contributed to creating this book. First and foremost, Cynthia Lamson, former Associate Director at Oceans Institute of Canada guided the process from its infancy, contributing her initiative, editorial skills and concern for the coastal environment.

Also involved in the initial process were Oliver Maas and John Somers. Pieter Jacobs assisted in the development, and Dr. Derek Davis and Alex Wilson of the Nova Scotia Museum offered commentary. Reg Miller provided advice and support. Ena Morris of the Oceans Institute of Canada assisted in formatting the original manuscript. Many other people along the way shared my enthusiasm for the project and a thank you to them collectively for helping me discover many special places.

Much of the natural history material for the book is from the *Natural History Map of Nova Scotia* by Derek S. Davis, Nova Scotia Museum, 1987, whose information is drawn largely from the *Natural History of Nova Scotia* by M. Simmons, D. Davis, L. Griffiths, and A. Muecke, Nova Scotia Departments of Education and Lands and Forests, 2 vols., 1984. For this book, the assistance of Fred Scott, Alex Wilson, Dale Smith and John Leduc is gratefully acknowledged. (These publications may be purchased at the Nova Scotia Museum, 1747 Summer St., Halifax, N.S. 902-424-7353.)

The Donner Canadian Foundation, the Canadian Employment and Immigration Commission (CEIC) and the Nova Scotia Department of Culture provided financial support.

Region: Bay of Fundy and Approaches 1.0

Evangeline and Glooscap Trails

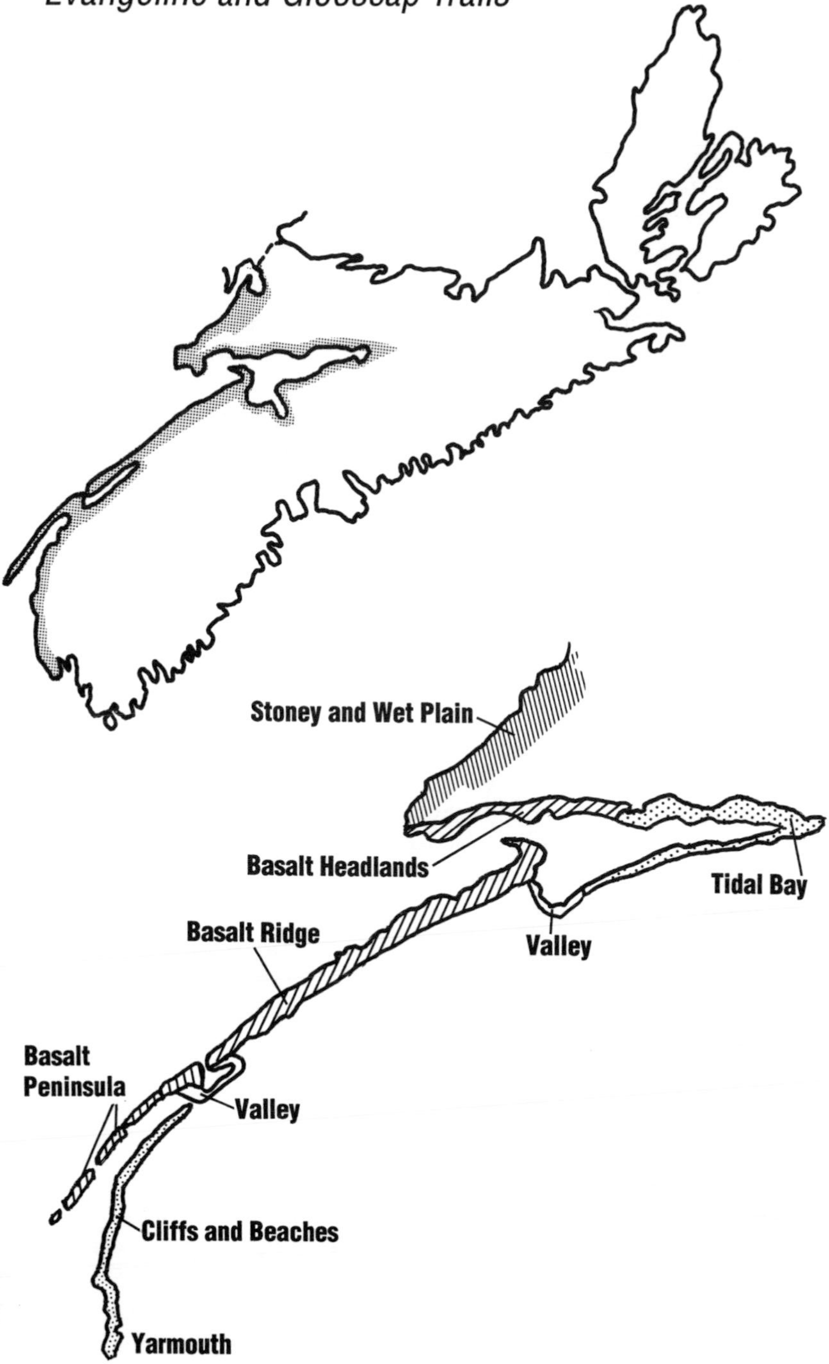

Stoney and Wet Plain
Basalt Headlands
Tidal Bay
Basalt Ridge
Valley
Basalt
Peninsula
Valley
Cliffs and Beaches
Yarmouth

The Bay of Fundy region is a marvellous phenomenon. Because of its funicular shape, the incoming tidal waters, as they flow from the Atlantic upward to the Minas Basin into Cobequid Bay, are forced into an ever smaller and smaller passageway. The force of the entering and exiting waters produce the highest tides in the world. Residents of the region acknowledge the impact these tides have had on their daily lives. From a passion for dulse (a salty seaweed), to a livelihood of clam digging or fishing, to an ability to swim in some of Nova Scotia's coldest waters, the people of the Bay of Fundy are salty, spunky, and in sync with the rhythm of the huge tides.

For over a century ambitious politicians have talked of harnessing this tidal power, but today people are beginning to understand the negative effect such projects can have on the environment.

Life along this coast is playful and hardy. The great mud flats provide feeding ground for migratory shore birds, while ancient crystallization and burial of extinct species offer up the riches rockhounds love to find. Cape Blomidon provides a majestic landmark for artists and nature lovers, and geologists and historians find this a rewarding region for the variety and scope of the formations, and the artifacts and records left behind.

The Bay of Fundy region in Nova Scotia is many things to many people. Here the first people of Nova Scotia, the Micmac, lived and travelled via both coastal and inland waterways, camping and feasting on Bay islands. Here the original French inhabitants, the Acadians, suffered the destruction of their lives in 1755 when the rich farmlands they had reclaimed from the sea by dyking were taken from them by the British. New England Planters developed the lands into profitable estates and United Empire and Black Loyalists journeyed here from the United States to begin new lives.

The Bay of Fundy and its Atlantic approach comprise the scenic Evangeline and Glooscap Trails. The region is divided into seven major areas representing distinctive geological characteristics: Cliffs and Beaches, the Basalt Peninsula, the Valley, the Basalt Ridge, the Tidal Bay, the Basalt Headlands, and the Stoney and Wet Plain. Each "theme area" suggests activities that take advantage of the natural features of each area.

1.1   Area: Yarmouth to Digby — Cliffs and Beaches

For the people of this area, the ocean shapes their lives. From Yarmouth on the craggy tip of southwest Nova Scotia to Digby Neck, the Atlantic Ocean's influence is all-pervasive.

This was once a rum-running and privateer coast where scoundrels and hustlers grew rich through illegal activity. It is also the land where displaced

Whale-watch, bird-watch, or climb the cliffs at Brier Island, a protected ecological site.

French Acadians eked out a new living from the sea after the explusion, and the Micmac saw their population almost wiped out by smallpox and encounters with Europeans. But this human history is brief compared to the history of the ancient landscape, shaped by glacial and volcanic activity.

In the recent geological past, the flexible crust of the earth tilted downward under the burden of a vast glacier. Nova Scotia was pressed into the earth, some areas being carried as much as 365 m (1200 ft) beneath the sea. The current fishing banks are the more elevated shoals of this drowned coastal plain. Rising seas, beginning about 10,000 years ago, continued to drown forests, erode headlands and drive salt marshes and beaches inland. The sandy beaches which dot the Bay of Fundy coasts were created from glacial deposits on the Scotian shelf being driven inwards by the sea as it rose during the postglacial period.

Tides in the bay are notorious and the dangerous squalls which rush in from the sea are a peril for fishing boats and their crews. Although the waters still provide good yearly yields of scallop, lobster and other inshore fish, the future of the Atlantic fishery is the subject of intense debate. Concerns about overfishing, species conservation, and habitat protection generate controversy about responsible resource management.

In Yarmouth, a 3.6 m (12 ft) tidal range rises to 4.8 m (16 ft) at St. Mary's Bay leaving fishing fleets floating at high tide and resting on mud at low tide. Yarmouth's history of shipping is commemorated in the exhibits at the Yarmouth County Historical Society Museum on Collins Street which also houses one of the largest collections of ship paintings in Canada. Manufacturing industries include fish processing plants, and the port is home to Atlantic Canada's largest herring fleet. The coast and marine waters around Yarmouth provide excellent seabird sighting possibilities. Historic Yarmouth Light, with a plaque commemorating this lighthouse's development, can be seen at Cape Fourchu.

In Port Maitland a left turn towards the breakwater leads to Sandy Cove Provincial Park (a day-use park). At Cape Cove (south of Cape St. Mary) there is a complete sequence of glacial tills from the last 120,000 years.

The district of Clare, midway between Yarmouth and Digby, is a distinctive Acadian community. The settlers, descended from the first Europeans to arrive in North America, arrived after the expulsion of 1755.

Mavillette Provincial Park provides beach access to an excellent area for shell collecting. There are about 250 species of shells in local waters, and nearly 100 of these may be found regularly on shore. The marsh behind the dunes is ideal for bird-watching. There is a large fossil spit exploited for gravel.

The beach at Bear Cove (near Meteghan) is worth visiting because of its fascinating escarpments and cliffs associated with legendary tales. The Gilbert

Cove lighthouse has been restored to its original state, and picnic grounds, overlooking the coast, are available.

Smuggler's Cove Provincial Park has a wonderful view of St. Mary's Bay. A rough path leads to a pebble beach and a natural cave. According to local legend, this cave was used to store contraband rum during Prohibition.

At Grosses Coques ("large clams") some of the largest clams on the eastern seaboard may be found. The clams were once so abundant that the first settlers survived by eating them throughout the long, cold winter. The blue slate beach at Major Point is a prime spot for many beach activities including swimming, sunning, and beachcombing.

From Meteghan River to Belliveau Cove, a glacial deposit of boulders and gravel forms a prominent ridge fronting the coast for 19.3 km (12 mi.) (best developed at Saulnierville). At Meteghan, a glaciomarine delta is upraised 19.8 m (65 ft) above high tide.

At Digby, whale-watching and deep-sea fishing can be arranged, and the famous Digby scallops are available at fish markets on the wharf or served in local restaurants.

Provincial parks in the area are located at Port Maitland Beach, Mavillette Beach, Smugglers Cove at Meteghan, Savary Park at Plympton, Bluff Head, Pembroke, Sand Beach, Cape Fourchu, and Kelley's Cove.

Activities: Mavillette Beach   1.1.1
Toss in a Wave, Look for Shells

In *Gifts of the Sea* Anne Morrow Lindbergh writes: "One never knows what chance treasures these easy unconscious rollers may toss up, on the smooth white sand of the conscious mind; what perfectly rounded stone, what rare shell from the ocean floor."

You may find such a treasure at Mavillette Beach, 33 km (20.5 mi.) northeast of Yarmouth, as nearly 100 species of local shells are found in these waters. (Before leaving Yarmouth, check at the county museum for display of local shells.)

Approximately 33 km (20.5 mi.) from Yarmouth on Route 1 at Cape St. Mary look for signs, to your left, to Mavillette Beach, a long stretch of fine white sand where you can beachcomb, and body surf in moderate waves. The park offers picnic facilities and walking trails. The highway from Yarmouth to Digby has been named "Canada's longest Main Street" because of the series of vibrant Acadian villages, dwarfed by giant churches, along its route where the eighteenth-century Acadian craftsmen left their mark after they settled in the area after 1755.

En route drop in to a local fishery for fresh fish. Sample the favourite local

Bay of Fundy and Approaches

Acadian dish, "rapure," a pie made from grated potatoes with the starch removed. In the 18th and 19th centuries, potato starch was used to stiffen clothing and this dish emerged as a frugal way of using up the remaining potato.

Return to Digby along Route 101 at Exit 28, where accommodation is available at Digby or Smith's Cove.

1.1.2   Map: Yarmouth to Mavillette

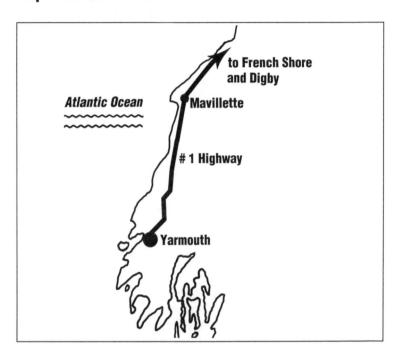

1.2   Area: Digby to Brier Island (Digby Neck) — Basalt Peninsula

After exploring the coast, the islands offshore become very intriguing. Digby Neck peninsula, stretching westerly out into the Atlantic, is formed from two thick lava flows, which created twin ridges with a central valley along the spine. The elevation decreases westwards, reaching sea level at Brier Island, and continues as rock ledges beyond. The land reemerges as Isle Haute in the upper Bay of Fundy, once a place where the Micmac held their feasts.

On the south side of Brier Island, near the entrance of the channel, columnar basalt cliffs descend in continuous steps far into the sea. At first glance the serrated ridges rising above the surface of the water look like piers defending the island. The rocky shores provide good substrate for seaweeds, including economically important dulse and Irish moss.

Storms from the south and east tear at the coastal spruce-fir forest while inland, sedge and sphagnum bogs on Brier Island contain rare and unusual plants such as Geum peckii, Betula michauxii, and Curly Grass Fern. Designated as a Canadian "Natural Heritage Area" because of its rich productive environment and abundant marine resources, Brier Island also contains southern (Virginian) species of intertidal flora which are rare or absent from the rest of the Maritimes.

Birds of prey, such as hawks and owls, are common on the island, and whale- and sea bird-watching may be arranged through island charter boat operators.

Public access to the shore for beachcombing and photography is provided through Central Grove Provincial Park, centre of Long Island on Route 217 and at Lake Midway.

Activities: Brier Island   1.2.1
Watch Whales, Climb Cliffs

To get to Brier Island from Digby, take Route 217 down the Basalt Peninsula known as "Digby Neck," a journey of approximately 75 km (46.6 mi.). You'll travel through the fishing communities of Tiverton, Freeport, and Westport, the latter two reached by ferry.

The Atlantic Ocean around the columnar basalt cliffs of Brier Island is rich with zooplankton brought to the surface by strong tidal currents. Here the fish, whales, and porpoises come to feed. First come the Fin and Minke Whales and Harbour Porpoises in early spring. Then, in late May and June, the Humpback Whales, followed in late June and July by the proliferation of Humpbacks and Atlantic White-Sided Dolphins. Whale-watching boat tours operate out of Tiverton and Westport.

The most diverse group of land and shore birds in the Bay of Fundy marine region is found here. At least three species of Shearwaters, the Atlantic Puffin, gannets, Razorbill Auks, Black Guillemots, Murres, several species of terns, Northern Fulmars, two species of Storm Petrels, and kittiwakes round out the most commonly sighted species.

A geological adventure awaits you on Brier Island in the form of large volcanic basalt columns. To get to the cliffs, take the secondary road to the eastern end of the island where a side road to the right leads to the beach. It is a moderate descent to the beach for a walk among the columns. Photographers will particularly enjoy the geometric uniqueness and subtle grey-blue pallor of the stones.

Bay of Fundy and Approaches

You may wish to return to Digby for golfing at the Digby Pines hotel, and to eat the area's specialty—scallops.

1.2.2   Map: Digby Neck and Islands

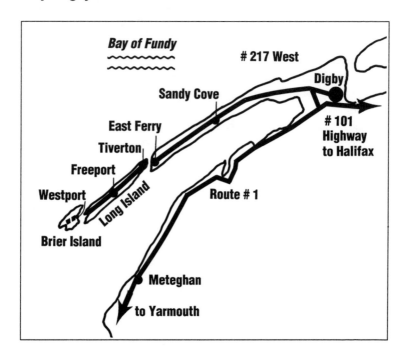

Bay of Fundy

217 West

Digby

Sandy Cove

East Ferry

Tiverton

Freeport

Westport

Long Island

Brier Island

Route # 1

101 Highway to Halifax

Meteghan

to Yarmouth

1.3   Area: Digby to Annapolis Royal and Wolfville to Cape Split — The Valley

Travelling west, you leave the granite and quartzite barrens of the Atlantic coast behind. The columnar basalt of Digby Neck, Long Island, and Brier Island changes into the sheltered area of the Annapolis Basin. The Micmac fished these shores four centuries ago before journeying inland, via Bear River and a complex lake, river, and portage system, to the Atlantic Ocean. They knew the journey well and gave the places names based on landscape features and personal experience. A modern day Micmac may tell you that Kejimkujik (home of the National Park) means "sore places" because, by the time they arrived in their canoes, derrières were hurting.

The Annapolis Basin area marks the beginning of a second region, the Triassic Lowlands. Soft sandstone, carved by river action and deepened by glacial scouring, forms an open-ended valley with material from the parent rock, while glacial and postglacial deposits provide a mixture of soil types. The North and South Mountains provide shelter which allows for the longest growing season in the province.

After the last glaciation 10,000 years ago, the sea rose quickly, eliminating some beaches and marine deltas while elevating shorelines and forming numerous sand spits and bars. Many of these formations are now high above sea level. At the east mouth of Bear River, sands may be seen 30.4 m (100 ft) above sea level and at Smith's Cove, a point is covered with fine sand 30.4 m (100 ft) above sea level. From Kingston to Greenwood, esker-like sand ridges created by the retreating sea can be observed.

The climate of the Basin area is moderated by marine influences and both fishing and farming activities are economically important. The way of life provided by the natural features of sea, beach, salt marsh, dykeland, and protected meadows include scallop fishing, clam digging, marsh grass harvesting, grain growing, and peach cultivating, all of which take place within a radius of twenty miles.

The Annapolis Basin and River provide important habitats for migrating waterfowl in spring and fall, but a variety of ducks remain throughout the winter. At the head of St. Mary's, shorebirds are often abundant, but August is the best month for observation.

Due to the high Fundy tides, coastal habitats consist of extensive intertidal areas, both salt marsh and mud flats, and associated dykelands. At the Historic Gardens in Annapolis Royal, you can walk along a path which divides a salt marsh and a dykeland and study a re-creation of an Acadian dykeland system. At Annapolis Royal, the town of firsts, the first dykeland in North America was built by French settlers.

The Annapolis area, with its strong agricultural base, attracts mammals and avifauna associated with farming including raccoons, red fox, woodchuck, skunk, muskrat, and mink. Pheasant, snipe, woodcock, and hawks are also present but crows are particularly common. The locality provides wintering habitat for bald eagles while the dykelands offer shelter to grey partridge (an endangered species) and short-eared owls.

Swimming, sailing, and beachcombing at Smith's Cove, clam digging on the mud flats of Upper Clements beaches, and canoe and boat rentals at Granville Ferry are among the many coastal recreational activities available. Beach access is available at Upper Clements Provincial Park.

The eastern end of the "Valley" district meets the Minas Basin and the "Tidal Bay" district of the Triassic Lowlands. The communities of Port Williams, Starr's Point, Kingsport, and Wolfville are under the "eye" of Cape Blomidon, the landmark end of the North Mountain range of the "Basalt Ridge" district. This coastal formation with its exposed red sandstone cliffs has been called an

Bay of Fundy
and Approaches

9

"animal" by poets. It is the legendary home of the Micmac god, Glooscap, and never ceases to inspire those who see it.

Kingsport and Wolfville were two of the three stops (the third being Parrsboro) for the ferry, *Kipawo*, which used to make a triangular journey between these points. The name was derived from the first two letters of each community. The ferry no longer carries people or cargo but is now a noted summer theatre which operates in Parrsboro. Parrsboro is also home to the new Nova Scotia Geological Museum (opening June 1993) with some 50 exhibits on the geology of the entire province and the significant crystal and fossil finds of the region. A shipbuilding theme site will open in 1994, a new development not to be missed by travellers. At Kingsport there is an excellent exposure of Triassic sandstone with fossil plant roots and rare dinosaur bones and tracks. At Wolfville raised beaches are present.

Traces of old Acadian dykes and roads are common throughout the area and early farming tools are often uncovered by local farmers. At Starr's Point you can walk from Prescott House along the Wellington Dyke (seven years and $100,000 to build).

Champlain sailed into the protective waters of the Annapolis Basin in 1605 looking for answers as to why his men had died the winter before. He got his answer, and a cure, from the Micmac who had thrived there for thousands of years: a steeped mixture of berries, barks, and roots—the formula to prevent scurvy. Unfortunately, the Micmac had no cure for the European disease, tuberculosis, which decimated their tribes.

1.3.1   Activities: Annapolis Royal
Walk "Town of Firsts," Golf amid Mud Flats,
Explore Plant Havens Galore

The Annapolis Royal area boasts two forts, walking tours of historic houses, a remarkable historic gardens complex, arts and antiques, and a golf course. Accommodations are well-managed and charming and the views are enhanced by three-hundred-year-old elms. The town has a refined calm, reminiscent of an earlier, more relaxed era.

Spend a day walking the town and the Historic Gardens before a 3 km (1.8 mi.) hike or ride to the Hillsdale Golf and Country club in nearby Allain's Creek with its impressive salt marsh. The golf course has just been enlarged to eighteen holes and borders the leisurely Annapolis River. You'll pass a grove of "elephant grass" on your left before the bridge. To the left is also the oldest Acadian dyke in the gardens property.

Bay of Fundy and Approaches

10

Map: Annapolis Royal   1.3.2

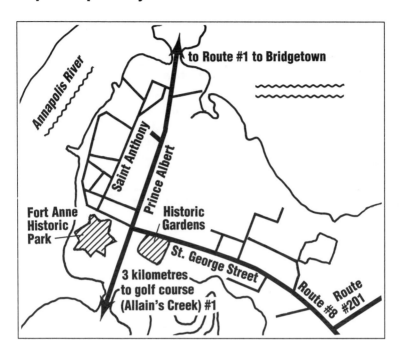

Activities: Wolfville   1.3.3
Cycle the Acadian Lands

Your cycling day begins in Wolfville, at the eastern end of the Annapolis Valley. The town bicycle store on Front Street will provide you with day or week rental if you don't have your own equipment. Just across the railway tracks, below the Anvil Tavern, you access the dyke where you will bear left travelling west to the village of Port Williams, about 3.5 km (2 mi.). Turn right in the village toward Starr's Point 5 km (3.1 mi.) where you can stop at the graceful gardens of the Prescott House for a morning snack. Bear right and continue north to Lower Canard and Porter Point, where, if the tide is out, you can engage in some therapeutic mud sliding, a "sport" that lets you revert to a primordial state. Wash off in the incoming tide and resume your more civilized posture on the bicycle. Continue on to Canning by backtracking to the first paved road 1 km (.6 mi.) at Lower Canard and head west (turn right at about 2 km (1.7 mi.) on Route 221 where a lovely Victorian tearoom—seventh house past the post office— promises to restore your decorum). After relaxing under lovely shade trees,

Bay of Fundy and Approaches

11

you will be ready for the inland ride through Canard back to Port Williams and Wolfville. A refreshing swim in the Gaspereau Valley will complete a truly wonderful day. In Wolfville, ask for directions to Lumsden Dam to wash off the salt, or shower at the Acadia University gymnasium (phone 902-542-2201).

If you prefer a longer tour, cycle east from Canning to Kingsport 6.5 km (4 mi.), north to North Medford 4 km (2.4 mi.) and right to Paddy's Island 1 km (.6 mi.) for a look at a small sandstone formation made by tide action. Backtrack to North Medford and continue straight (west) to North Corner 3.5 km (2 mi.) where you turn left to Pereaux and on to Canning 5.5 km (3.4 mi.).

For more bicycle trips, contact Bicycle Nova Scotia, Box 3010 South, Halifax, N.S. B3J 3G6, or obtain Gary Conrod's comprehensive book on cycling.

1.3.4   Activities: Blomidon Park and Cape Split
Two Days Hiking

Some challenging hiking awaits you on the outer peninsula of Cape Blomidon, where the basalt-covered sandstone of the North Mountain range shows its red undercoat. The cliffs of Blomidon, though unscalable, even for an experienced rock climber, are viewable from the hike atop Blomidon.

Both hikes are approximately 17 km (10.5 mi.) so you may want a recovery day in-between if you plan to do both. Tenting is available at Blomidon Provincial Park from where you will begin the first day's hike. If you're not camping, many wonderful Bed and Breakfast Inns, featuring the Planters and the Victorian eras, operate in Canning, Wolfville, and Starr's Point.

The first day's hike will take you along the top of Cape Blomidon, which overlooks the falling sandstone of the eroding cliffs. If you are there in June the red trillium will be in bloom and you may see a hawk or eagle flying silently below you. The hike is marked and continues in a loop back through woodlands given to the people by R.A. Jodrey, the gypsum and industrial king of Hantsport.

The second hike to Cape Split begins as a drive or a bike ride from Blomidon Provincial Park to Scots Bay on the other side of the peninsula, a distance of about 21 km (13 mi.). Backtrack from the park to Blomidon about 7 km (4.3 mi.) and turn right onto a dirt road where the sign reads "Look-off." Turn right at Junction 358 and go 14 km (4.7 mi.) to the very end of the road where the hike begins. It's 8.5 km (5.3 mi.) through coniferous and deciduous forest to the grassy knoll at the end.

Cape Split is surrounded by two seas, the Minas Channel and the Minas Basin. Extreme caution must be exercised when hiking toward this headland. There are no barriers protecting you from the beach some hundred metres

Hiking in the deciduous forest near Cape Split.

below and there is only one sign warning you of the danger. At several points toward the end, the path diverges to the edge and one slip could be fatal. The earth at the end of the split is also very unstable as it is in the latter stages of erosion so don't mistake a precarious overhang for solid ground. Despite these hazards, Cape Split offers a spectacular view unlike any other in Nova Scotia.

1.3.5   Map: Wolfville to Cape Split

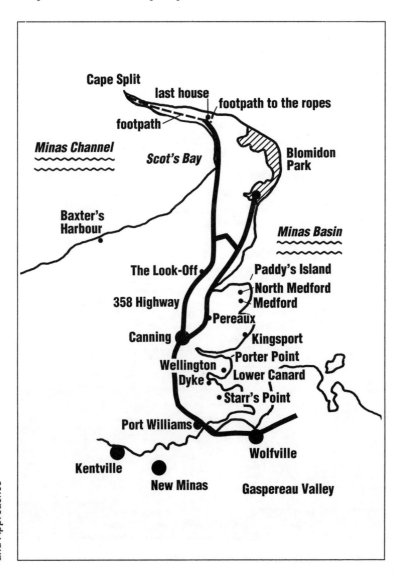

Area: Delap's Cove to Scot's Bay (Fundy Shore)   1.4
— Basalt Ridge

When you leave the salt marsh and mud flat area of the Annapolis Basin and travel over the North Mountain range, you find yourself along a rugged, rocky shore where the incredible tides range from a slim trickle at ebb to a swelling surge at high tide.

If you decide to pick mussels at Morden, you will see a stone cross monument at the site where, in 1755, Acadians expelled by the British hid from the soldiers during the winter, surviving on mussels and fresh meat provided by the Micmac. Visit the church here, built in 1790, its walls plastered with powdered mussel shells.

A hiking trail at Delap's Cove offers a unique opportunity to experience the smell of salt air mixed with spruce woods.

Along the Fundy Coast ride eastward, you will see (if the day is clear) a great view of Cape Split jutting out into the Bay. A day or so later you could be hiking the 12.9 km (8 mi.) woodland trail to the end of "the Split," an important ecological site.

When the continents drifted apart some 200 million years ago, rifts opened in the sandy plain between the Cobequid Hills (Truro area) and South Mountain, and basaltic lavas welled up spreading over the area. The North Mountain ridge was created when the lavas cooled causing fractures, tilting and offsets in the basalt.

Some of Nova Scotia's most dramatic scenery is found on North Mountain, particularly at Cape Blomidon where Cape Split sweeps around into the Minas Basin. The section of shore from St. Croix Cove to Cape Split provides a rich ground for collecting crystals of amethyst, cornelian and moss agates, jasper and hornstone, bloodstone and spar.

Wind gaps through the ridge are found at Parker's Cove and Delap's Cove. These are the abandoned lower valleys of rivers which flowed from central Nova Scotia into the present bay and were eventually captured by the Annapolis River. Digby Gut is the drowned lower valley of Bear River.

Smooth egg-shaped rocks cover the beach at Hampton while, at Baxter's Harbour, black, rough platforms of hardened lava form an unusual rocky shoreline.

The vegetation of the "Basalt Ridge" is a transition zone where coastal red spruce is abundant but beech and sugar maple are also found at higher elevations. On exposed basalt cliffs, such as at Cape Split, arctic-alpine plant communities are found. Cliff-top forests are of the true coastal type, pure stands of evergreens, but become, within a few feet, open hardwood forest.

This area supports a deer population, but few bear or bobcat. The Ridge

Bay of Fundy
and Approaches

gives a funnelling effect to the movements of migratory birds, particularly hawks and owls, as they head towards Brier Island in the fall. The same is true for bat migrations crossing the Bay of Fundy en route to their wintering area. The exposed basalt along the shoreline provides good habitat for molluscs and crustaceans, especially near wharves where lobster traps have been emptied.

Recreational opportunities along the "Basalt Ridge" range from hiking to sea kayaking, swimming to bay cruises, rock hounding to the art of eating lobster. Experienced rock climbers will find the cliffs challenging.

Visitors should be aware of the power of the tide, which moves rapidly and can catch one off guard. Kayakers have also been caught in the Bay's fierce whirlpools and the rip tides off Cape Split.

Provincial parks are located at Cottage Cove, northwest of Middleton, Valley View, Scots Bay, Blomidon, and Baxter's Harbour.

1.4.1   Activities: Delap's Cove
Walk along the Fundy Shore

When it's sweltering in the Valley, the Bay of Fundy beckons with cool, moist breezes. Valley residents have, over the centuries, enjoyed the benefits of being only 10 km (6 mi.) from "over the mountain" where some of the most interesting geology in Nova Scotia can be found. Volcanic lava hardened into basalt crystals, carved and worn by the ever present tidal waters, creates unusual shore surfaces at Baxter's Harbour, north of Canning and round smooth beach stones at Hampton, north of Bridgetown.

Although a road runs near the Fundy Shore all the way from Delap's Cove to Scots Bay, it is not a direct route. It zigzags along the ridge and down into the harbour communities. If you are travelling at a slow pace, you can drive the length of the region in a day, stopping in the various communities to explore beaches and sample lobster and dulse.

On leaving Annapolis Royal (it's a good idea to pack a picnic lunch), cross the causeway, turning left toward Port Royal. Just before Port Royal (where you can visit a replica of a seventeenth century French fort), turn right to go over the mountain to Delap's Cove. Go 6 km (3.7 mi.) to the T in the road, turn left and it's a short distance to the beginning of the Delap's Cove Wilderness Trail. Allow at least two and a half hours for the hike along the rocky shore and through the woods. Maps for the trip are available at the beginning of the trail.

After a hike and a picnic, backtrack to the T and continue east to Parker's Cove, Young's Cove, Phinney Cove, and Hampton where you'll see the oval stones. Continue along the shore to St. Croix Cove and Port Lorne or head inland to take either Routes 221 through farm country or Route 1 through the chain of Valley towns; both routes lead to Cape Blomidon.

Map: Annapolis Royal to Scot's Bay   1.4.2

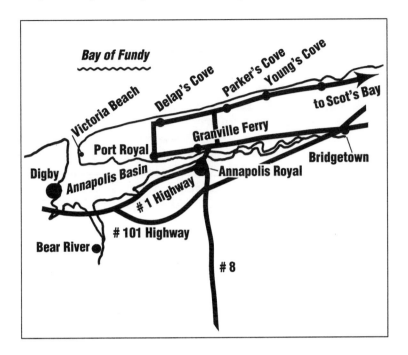

Area: Wolfville to Economy (Minas Basin) — Tidal Bay   1.5

At the eastern end of the Bay of Fundy, the shoreline contracts and forms the Minas Basin, which continues easterly as the slender Cobequid Bay. The Bay ends at the mouth of the Salmon River at Truro. Walls of sea water, known as "tidal bores," rush up river mouths repeating a daily merger of salt and fresh water. These perpetual tides are an extraordinary phenomenon which the locals discuss routinely, along with the more universal topic of weather.

The western shores of the Minas Basin form the eastern end of the Valley district of the Triassic Lowlands. Excellent displays of exposed sandstone can be seen in the red cliffs of Blomidon. The rest of the Minas Basin and Cobequid Bay is referred to as the "Tidal Bay" district of the Triassic Lowlands. Carved out by rivers which eroded eastward from the Bay of Fundy, the area has cut a channel along the Minas Passage Fault between Cape Split and Cape Sharp. Repeated glaciations have shaped the Bay and given it its distinctive profile.

The sea has been rising slowly for several millennia. Measurements in the outer reaches of the Fundy coast indicate that changes have taken place at a

Bay of Fundy and Approaches

rate of approximately 40.6 cm (16 in) per 100 years. In addition, rapid erosion of soft surface rocks, accelerated by rising seas, resulted in enormous volumes of sediment being deposited in river estuaries. Sand bars, notably in the Avon and Shubenacadie Rivers, offer visible testimony of such coastal dynamics.

Around Cobequid Bay, which includes the south Noel Shore side, the Triassic red rock beds are nearly horizontal and form a low area with gentle undulations. At Walton, you can observe the Triassic sandstones above vertical red siltstones which are exposed at low tide.

Coastal marshes are also being eroded as the coastline retreats. In some places the remains of fossil forests of beech, pine, black spruce, and larch are exposed. These trees were buried by bluish marine clay and boggy marsh when rising seas and an expanded tidal range carried salt water up low-lying river valleys and over coastal lowlands. Once exposed to tidal action, the fossil stumps are quickly destroyed; however, new ones are continuously being exhumed.

The extensively farmed soils in this area are heavier than soils found in the "Valley" district. Scattered sugar maple, beech, and yellow birch occur locally on low ridges, but spruce, fir, white birch, red maple, hemlock, and white pine dominate other sites. Red maple and white birch replace red oak as post-fire species. White spruce, red spruce, and balsam fir are the usual invaders of old fields. Heathlands with jack pine are found in the Debert area, and the Minas Basin is fringed by salt marshes.

The "Tidal Bay" district provides a mix of forest, open land, and intertidal habitats. In late summer and early fall large concentrations of shore birds and moderate numbers of waterfowl assemble on the south coast of the Minas Basin and in Cobequid Bay. Evangeline Beach (part of the "Valley" district of the Triassic Lowlands) is a staging and feeding area for hundreds of thousands of migratory shore birds. Many species of sandpiper and plover can be observed scurrying over the sand or taking flight in nervous masses. Bald eagles nest along the river at Caddell Rapids and elsewhere. In addition, the shallow, muddy water plus warm summers and cold winters make the waters a hospitable habitat for many interesting marine animals.

Tidal bores occur in rivers flowing into the Bay of Fundy. The best examples in Nova Scotia occur in the Salmon and Avon Rivers. The look-off at the Shubenacadie Tidal Bore Park offers an ideal view. Other good tidal bore sites are located at Maccan, River Hebert, Lower Maccan, Truro, and Walton.

Noel was once the site of a prosperous Acadian village. The remains of Acadian dykes are still visible from East Noel, where a small, shaded rest area provides a viewing location. The district was resettled in 1762 by families from Northern Ireland. An interesting legend credits the infamous Captain Kidd with bringing his pirate ship to Sloop Rock (off Noel) to be remasted. It is said the

Bay of Fundy
and Approaches

Captain threw out bars of silver as payment, but those who supplied the timber would not touch pirate silver and the bars were left on the reef to be covered up by mud.

To the right at Noel, a loop leads to Burncoat Head, the point at which the highest tides in the world have been recorded. The greatest measured distance between high and low tide here is 16.6 m (54 ft). Guided tours are available to view this phenomenon in safety. The beach is a feeding place for thousands of migratory shore birds in spring and fall.

At Maitland, where the largest wooden ship, the *W.D. Lawrence* was built, you can visit Lawrence House, a provincial museum which houses artifacts and memorabilia about this ship. Across from the museum, you can watch the tidal bore from the Maitland Picnic Look-off. Nearby is a marsh developed by Ducks Unlimited, a non-profit organization devoted to preserving wildfowl habitat.

Economy, from the Micmac word "Kenomee," meaning "a long point jutting out into the sea," marks the division between Minas Basin and Cobequid Bay; the Micmac word "Cobequid" means "the end of flowing waters." At Economy, the clams are touted as the world's best, and striped bass fishing is still enjoyed at Bass River.

Located at Highland Village is a dyke sluice believed to be over 200 years old, which was once used by Acadians to drain their marshes.

Great Village was once an important shipbuilding community and port of call from 1817 to 1891. You can see remnants of the craft in the many fine old mansions formerly owned by sea captains.

At Debert, replicas of arrowheads from a 10,000 year old paleoindian community can be viewed at the Debert Development office. Thousands of artifacts, including scrapers, flake chips, darts, needles, awls, gravers, and hammer stones have been found here.

Public access to the beach at Anthony Provincial Park at Maitland provides an opportunity to see the variation between high and low tide. An exposed area of red sand at low tide offers a great chance to walk and wade in warm water.

Activities: Avonport and Evangeline Beach   1.5.1
Observe the Tidal Bore, Swim in the Land of Red Mud

Welcome to the heart of Blomidon country and a full day of play near Minas Basin's shores. Sip wine made from Annapolis Valley grapes and eat succulent lobster sandwiches, accompanied by tea served in china cups. Watch tens of thousands of shore birds dart and sweep in a silvery wave over red mud flats, or gaze at the magnificence of Cape Blomidon against the green salt marsh grass and the blue sky. Discover the prints of dinosaurs in the rocks of the

Bay of Fundy and Approaches

eroding shoreline by the Avon River, and observe the tide race up its bed—all this within a ten kilometre radius.

From Wolfville, travel east along Route 1 to Grand Pré where you can dine at the Evangeline Tea Room whose menu has not changed since the 1940s. It's the only eating establishment in the province that gives you extra hot water for your tea without asking, and one of the few that still serves up the metal milkshake maker with the glass. Sample wonderful homemade fruit pies in season, apple, rhubarb, strawberry, cherry, and peach. The chowder and the scones are from traditional recipes, and the books in the china shop can fill you in on the local history.

Continue east on Route 1 and 101 to Avonport (Exit 9) where a short drive past the school along the Bluff Road brings you to Avonport Beach. (Cross the railway tracks, and, at the barn, a short dirt road to your left leads to the beach.) A walk to the right past the cliffs will bring you to the shore where rocks containing fossils can be found.

The prominent landmark of this area is, of course, Cape Blomidon, which was and is the spiritual home of the Micmac god, Glooscap. According to legend, Glooscap came mysteriously out of the west to live with the Micmac, whom he called the "children of light." He made his home on Blomidon where he lived with his grandmother, Nogami, and Marten, his servant. It is said that true believers can still see the footprints of Glooscap on the red cliffs and that the mist which sometimes rises from the Basin's waters is the steam caused by Nogami and Marten quenching their cooking fires. Glooscap is a benevolent spirit who carefully watches over his people but is never seen. His voice is in the wind. As he turns, so the wind blows. His anger is the thunder and the raging waves. His pleasure is the sunlight, and when Glooscap sleeps, each flower and leaf is still.

After your meditation of Blomidon and a swim at the beach in the warming waters of high tide, backtrack to Grand Pré and visit the winery. Then on to the National Park at Grand Pré, the centre for preserving Acadian history. The guides here are expertly informed on Acadian genealogy, and Acadian people from all over North America, particularly from the Atlantic provinces and the southern US (Louisiana "cajuns") come here annually to trace their roots and to contemplate the past struggles of their ancestors. Continue on to Evangeline Beach, where, if you're visiting in late August or September, you may see the shore birds—willetts, Greater and Lesser Yellow Legs, plovers, and sandpipers feeding before their migration south. Stay at Evangeline Beach for a picnic and camp or travel back to Grand Pré for a lobster supper and a stay at one of the bed and breakfasts in the area.

Map: Avon River Area   1.5.2

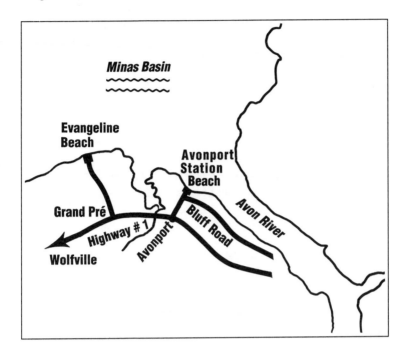

Activities: Maitland and Bass River   1.5.3
Ride the Tidal Bore and Fish for Striped Bass

Cobequid Bay, the narrow part of the funnel of Minas Basin, is the site of tidal bore rafting, a recreational activity unique to the region. To get to the "rafts" at the mouth of the Shubenacadie River, travel east from Wolfville on Route 1 to Windsor and take Route 14 east to Brooklyn, turning left onto Route 215 to the Noel Shore. Continue until Selma where the proprietors of the local bed and breakfast can fill you in on rafting details.

After an exciting "sail" up the river on the rising crest of the tidal bore, travel to Truro (Route 236 at South Maitland where you'll connect to Route 2 to Parrsboro), which will take you along the other side of Cobequid Bay and Minas Basin to see Blomidon's other profile. You'll pass through Great Village where you can visit a general store museum which re-creates shopping styles of 1874. The next village, Portapique, features a large sandy beach ideal for beachcombing or sunbathing (take the gravel road to your left to reach the beach).

Bay of Fundy
and Approaches

When you arrive at Bass River, inquire about fishing licenses at the local store before casting your line in the mouth of Bass River. Although the freshwater fish population of Nova Scotia has diminished greatly over the last twenty years, trout can still be found here. Local organizations are continuing to investigate the causes of the decline of fish stocks and are pressuring governments for environmental protection.

After you've caught your quota, set out for the Parrsboro Shore with its splendid Five Islands Provincial Park where red, eroded sandstone formations look like sergeants-at-arms, worn by the war with the sea. Here hiking trails and interpretive displays will inform you of the geology and legends of the area.

Parrsboro has been placed on the world map because of its important fossil find of *Trithelodont,* a mammal-like reptile which provides crucial evidence about the origin of mammals. The new Geological Museum has exhibits showing this and other fossil finds.

You can camp at Five Islands after a day fishing and fossil-hunting.

Riding the tidal bore on the Shubenacadie River.

Bay of Fundy
and Approaches

Map: Wolfville to Bass River   1.5.4

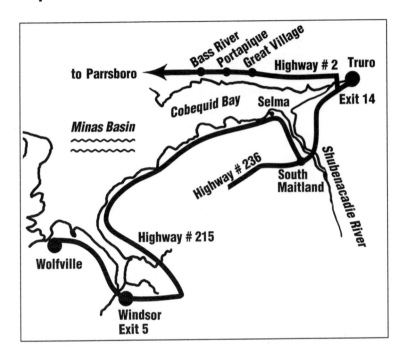

Area: Parrsboro to Advocate Harbour   1.6
— Basalt Headlands

If you are travelling along the North Mountain "Basalt Ridge" on a clear day, you can see the north shore of Minas Basin and Parrsboro across the Minas Channel. The Fundy Coast region from Economy to Advocate Harbour is called the "Basalt Headlands" and is a continuation of the Glooscap Trail.

Legend says that Glooscap created the Five Islands by throwing handfuls of sod at Beaver, who had mocked his magical powers. Near Advocate is Glooscap's "Three Sisters," a treacherous rock formation that requires caution when visiting because of the rapid tides.

Parallel faults, juxtaposed basalts, and erodable sandstones create a varied landscape of hills and lowlands, cliffs and headlands where mineral deposits and fossil remains provide added geological interest.

From Economy to Partridge Island the hilly landscape reflects the contrasting resistance to erosion of basalt and the Triassic sandstones. Slopes capped with basalt are Portapique Mountain 152.4 m (500 ft), Economy Mountain

Bay of Fundy and Approaches

243.8 m (800 ft) and Spencer's Island 152.4 m (500 ft). The high sandstone cliffs at Five Islands Park, and on the islands themselves, exist because of the resistant basalt. Another prominent headland, Cape Chignecto, is formed from granite and is the most westerly extremity of the Cobequid Hills. Some of the high basalt-capped blocks have cliffs with columnar jointing: Partridge Island, Cape Sharp, and Spencer's Island. Semiprecious stones are found in the amygdaloidal basalts at Partridge Island.

Exposed Triassic sandstone is easily eroded. At Lower Economy a tidal platform over 1.6 km (1 mi.) wide has been cut on the coastal exposure by waves. The low Triassic area immediately north of Cape d'Or will eventually be worn away leaving the basalt-capped sediments as stacks, similar to Five Islands.

Younger sediments, Jurassic in age, containing dinosaur bones and footprints have been found near the village of Five Islands. Under the "Special Places Protection Act," the public is not permitted to dig fossils without a permit, but if you find a loose fossil on the beach, it is yours to keep. The Nova Scotia Museum in Halifax can help you identify your find. Fossils still embedded in the bedrock must be left alone. Only people with a Heritage Research Permit may collect fossils still attached to solid bedrock. It is important to heed this law, not only because it *is* the law but because once a site is disturbed by digging, it cannot be restored to an undisturbed state.

Fossils are critical geological evidence and document changes in local climate and morphology. Scientists need to know the sequence of species and the position of fossils above or below one another reveals this information. A professional "dig" involves several people working meticulously with tools as small as spoons and paintbrushes. The whole site is mapped with a grid of lines, and the precise location of each object is recorded. Usually there is only one chance to record this vital information.

Large glacial outwash deposits are common along the Parrsboro shore. The town of Advocate is built upon an outwash plain. The harbour is enclosed by a sand bar and cobble beaches derived from gravels eroded from the outwash deposits.

The coastal forest changes as the climate changes from maritime to continental. Spruce, hemlock, and pine forests with hardwoods are found, together with the pure stands of common spruce, fir, and pine forest. Pure stands of white spruce are found in old fields. The exposed cliffs at Cape d'Or, an important ecological site, provide habitat for arctic alpine plant species.

Deer coming down from the Cobequids winter along this shore. Islands provide breeding areas for the Double-crested Cormorant, Common Eider, Great Blue Heron, Herring Gull and Black-backed Gull. At Advocate Harbour, tidal flats and salt marshes attract some migratory shore birds and waterfowl.

Bay of Fundy and Approaches

Sites of special interest include the Economy Mountain Look-off where, to the north and west, you can see the steep escarpment of the Cobequid fault, and in the foreground, low-lying Carboniferous and Triassic sediments. Moose River is a unique ecological site where a mature red spruce forest grows. Five Islands Provincial Park contains dinosaur bones and footprints, and at Moose Island you can see agate and basalt sea stacks. On Partridge Island semiprecious minerals can be found, and Advocate boasts raised beaches 35 m (115 ft) above high water.

The picturesque rock formation of Cape Split, across the Minas Channel, can be seen from the highway approaching Fox River.

It was near Spencer's Island that the mystery ship, the brigantine *Mary Celeste,* was built in 1861. In 1872, she left New York City bound for Genoa. Some weeks later the Nova Scotia brig *Dei Gratia* came upon the *Mary Celeste* drifting erratically. Upon boarding the ship, the rescuers realized that no one was aboard. All sail was set and not a rope was out of place. Only the ship's papers and the chronometer were missing. No storms had been reported and the *Mary Celeste* was watertight. No survivors were ever found.

Spencer's Island is an island in name only. A short distance from its excellent beach, and within easy reach, is Glooscap's Kettle, a small island shaped exactly like an overturned pot or kettle, formed from tidal action on the sandstone.

You may visit the lighthouse at Cape d'Or, located on a steep hill.

Advocate Harbour is historically linked to a group of Belleisle Acadians, creators of the famous dykelands near the Annapolis Basin. After their expulsion in 1755, this group of Acadian refugees, aided by the Micmac, sailed across the Bay and settled at a place which came to be known as Refugee Cove.

The Three Sisters formation near Advocate is an excellent place for clam digging and driftwood and rock collecting.

Parrsboro holds an annual "Rockhound Roundup" in August with displays, demonstrations, and boat tours. The dramatic effect of the tides can be observed at the wharf when fishing boats and lumber freighters are left stranded high and dry at low tide. At high tide, water fills the harbour and reaches the mouth of the small creek that runs under the main street.

The Geological Mineral and Gem Museum features a fascinating collection of the dinosaur fossils, semiprecious gems, and minerals that have been found on the Parrsboro shores. The shores of the Minas Basin in this area have thousands of prehistoric footprints that record a parade of creatures, including the rare reptiles most closely related to mammals.

Ottawa House is the former home of Sir Charles Tupper, a distinguished Nova Scotia politician and Canadian prime minister. From the veranda you can

Bay of Fundy
and Approaches

see Partridge Island, which is now joined to the mainland. In 1869, during a ferocious storm known as the Saxby Gale, waves drove the beach inland, creating a large sand bar that connected the island to the mainland.

1.6.1   Activities: Advocate Harbour
Kayak, Collect Rocks

Advocate Harbour allows the serious rock hound the potential to find semiprecious stones, while watching the rise and fall of 15 m (50 ft) tides. If you want to get away from shore, this area is a good place for a sea kayaking adventure. Contact Scott Cunningham, one of Nova Scotia's most experienced sea kayakers for details of planned expeditions (Tel. 902-772-2774).

But for those who prefer to stay on land, Advocate Harbour, (specifically, near Horseshoe Cove) has many interesting pebbles on its beach, some dark brown and white, which are jasper agate, often stained brown from mud and iron compounds. The more reddish this crystal becomes, the closer it is to carnelian, a good find. On the east side of the Cove, the basalt is solidified into pillow basalt filled with a clear agate flecked with small red dots.

Toward Advocate you can find copper along the shoreline. At the turn of the century, a copper mine operated here and a company town of about a dozen cottages was built. On the eastern hillside sloping down to the cove, a path takes you to the old workings. Be careful walking here for old shafts are hidden underbush.

Kayaking among rock sentinals in the Basalt Headlands.

Since the tides predominate in this region, it is helpful to know their times so as not to be caught out too far on the beach when the waters rush in, as they inevitably do. For tide times, call DIAL-A-TIDE (426-5494).

Map: Parrsboro to Advocate Harbour   1.6.2

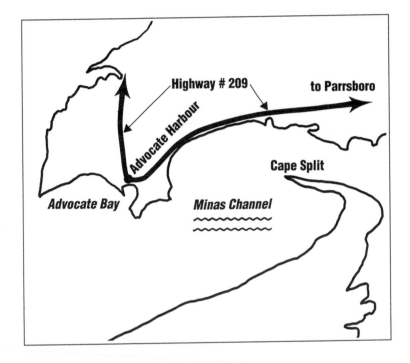

Area: Advocate Harbour to Amherst (Chignecto Bay Area)   1.7
— Stoney and Wet Plain

Off the beaten track, even by Nova Scotian standards, is the coastline of Chignecto Bay, the "Chignecto Plains" district of the Carboniferous Lowland region. Giant ferns once flourished in extensive wetlands here, and compressed remains of the plant material, coal seams, marbling the layers of shale and grey sandstone, can be seen in shoreline outcrops. In other veins, gypsum salt and limestone rise through the strata reminding observers of an even earlier time when a marine basin covered the plain.

This area marks a crossover to a part of Nova Scotia formed at a different time and place from the other districts in the Bay of Fundy and Approaches area. Earth scientists believe that present-day Nova Scotia is a product of two

Bay of Fundy
and Approaches

27

terranes (the Avalon and Meguma Terranes) of entirely different rock types, formed in different time periods and at a considerable distance from one another. Through the process of plate tectonics, the slow, inexorable movement of sections of the earth's crust, these two terranes merged to form the foundations of Nova Scotia.

As they drifted toward North America, about 400 million years ago, a series of collisions occurred, producing the Appalachian mountain chain.

During the Carboniferous period (360-290 million years ago) the mountain chains, thought to have once been at least as high as the Alps, were severely eroded by active river systems. Seas rose, precipitating the large quantities of salt, gypsum, anhydrite, and limestone found in the lower carboniferous rocks. As the seas retreated, enormous swamps were formed, dominated by huge ferns and providing a habitat for amphibians and the earliest reptiles. The region's coal deposits were formed during this period, as were many of the fossils which can be seen today in the exposed cliffs of Joggins, overlooking the entrance to the Cumberland Basin.

From Joggins to Maccan and Springhill, the luxuriant growth of tree ferns and seed ferns resulted in the formation of up to 70 coal seams with the thickest ones near Joggins. The main seam at Joggins is 1.2 m (4 ft) thick. Mining disasters resulting in the loss of hundreds of lives at nearby Springhill attest to the fact that these seams formed in an unstable environment.

Near Joggins there is a classic coastal section of late Carboniferous strata. Between Coal Mine Point and Lower Cove, tree stumps of *Calamites* and *Sigillaria* can be seen in their original growth positions. Siltstones rich in plant debris, and limestones containing the shells of freshwater and brackish water pelecypods and ostracods occur. Amphibian and reptile bones and the tracks of giant arthropods have also been found.

These exceptional shoreline exposures have drawn geologists to the area since the mid-nineteenth century when Sir Charles Lyell, the founder of modern geology, wrote, "I have never travelled in any country where my scientific pursuits were better understood or were more zealously forwarded than in Nova Scotia."

Coal was mined at Joggins for many years and there are records of coal sales to Boston as early as 1720. At peak production, the local mines had a yearly output of 100,000 tons.

The district offers prime moose and deer, and good bear habitat. Raccoons are found near the scattered agricultural settlements. Beaver densities are low. The Maccan marshes are significant for waterfowl breeding and are part of the important Cumberland Basin region.

Immense deposits of rock salt are being worked by means of deep brining wells just north of Nappan.

The tidal bore may be seen from the Maccan River and River Hebert bridges. A Miners' Memorial Museum shows the lifestyle and working conditions of coal miners in the River Hebert area.

A road from River Hebert leads to Minudie. Before 1755, when the British captured the French Fort Beausejour on the Chignecto Isthmus, Minudie used to be an Acadian settlement. The inhabitants didn't want to participate in raids against the English and kept to themselves. However, in 1755, New Englanders raided the village and destroyed it, killing many people and taking the survivors as prisoners. After the Deportation in 1755, the land was granted to S.F.W. DesBarres. Many Acadians were then resettled on the property as tenant farmers. Amos Seaman bought the estate in the mid-1800s. He quarried rock for grindstones locally and established a large store at the Minudie wharf and made a fortune trading between Boston and the West Indies. "King" Seaman built a mansion at Minudie and also maintained another fine home in Boston. A school in the town attests to his influence.

Activities: Joggins
Fossil Hunting

If you continue along Route 209 past Advocate Harbour, you will cross Cape Chignecto and eventually arrive at Joggins. This is a special place of geological formations and fossil finds. The coast of the Cape is not reachable by land but provides probably the most spectacular coastal scenery in Nova Scotia and can be sea kayaked with great pleasure. (Contact Coastal Adventures in Tangier for more information.)

Signs of the now-defunct Joggins coal mining industry can be seen in the streets lined with company houses, built specifically for the miners and their families.

A short distance away, along a shale-strewn beach, are the eroding cliffs of Joggins where fossils from 300 million years ago are easily found. Joggins' fossil cliffs can be reached by following the signs visible from the main area of the village. They lead to the shore where your walk begins.

Laing Ferguson, in his book *The Fossil Cliffs of Joggins,* writes that, "These rivers (of 300 million years ago) meandered across jungle-or-forest-covered plains inhabited by salamander-like amphibians and lizard-like reptiles, as well as by *Arthropleura*, a fascinating creature, that looked like a giant sowbug, about 2 metres long. The most obvious fossils that you will see in the cliffs at Joggins are the tree stumps, ancestors of our present day club mosses and the horsetail plant. Joggins is especially unique for the fossils of amphibians and aquatic reptiles found in the tree trunks, preserved as they fell from the ravages there as if in insulated, tightly-packed tubes, the trunks. The visible coal seams

Bay of Fundy and Approaches

29

1.7.2   **Map: Joggins**

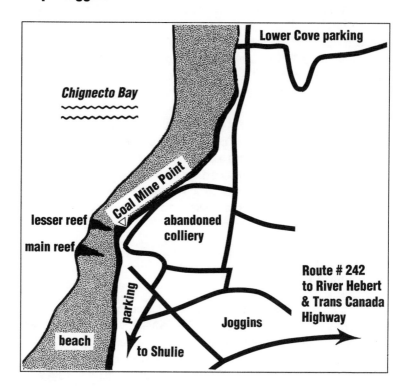

are also the remains of plant life, preserved as coal rather than as a drowned forest, due to a slower process".

The walk along the cliffs between Lower Cove and Coal Mine Point is approximately 3 km (1.9 mi.) and you can visit a private display in a house along the road. Some local people like to show off their favourite fossils, accompanied by coal mining stories.

Rock falls are frequent, due to the cliffs being battered by waves at high tide. Don't get too close to the overhangs, especially in the spring when erosion is most likely to occur. The best time to visit the cliffs is during the three hours before and after low tide, preferably when low tide occurs after the sun is up and the rocks have dried. Consult tide tables so you can paln to have several hours on the shore before the tide returns.

As you wander along the shore, remind yourself that some of the first reptiles on earth walked eons ago here beneath towering trees.

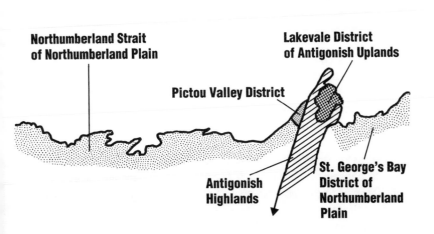

Northumberland Strait of Northumberland Plain

Lakevale District of Antigonish Uplands

Pictou Valley District

Antigonish Highlands

St. George's Bay District of Northumberland Plain

The Northumberland Shore, an area of warm salt waters and straight sandstone cliffs, has teriffic beaches, festivals, good eating, great cycling and touring, and offers a meditative ambience found no where else in the province. This is the coast which Scottish, Portuguese and French Hugenots settled in the 18th and 19th centuries and their descendents proliferate the communities here, making the area a lively mix of Scottish, Portuguese, and French, as well as other ethnic blood ties.

It comprises the "Sunrise Trail" as described in tourist guides, and includes two natural history theme districts of the Carboniferous Lowland Region—the Coastal Plain, and Hills and Valleys.

The Northumberland Plain area stretches from Amherst to Arisaig and St. Georges Bay to Havre Boucher.

The Hills and Valleys district, from McArras Brook to Arisaig, is described as the Pictou Valley, while the coastal area from Malignant Cove to Lakevale is referred to as the Antigonish Uplands.

2.1   Area: Amherst to Arisaig — Northumberland Plain

The Northumberland Strait area consists of fine red sandstones shaped into broad folds by the earth's pressure. Gypsum outcrops and salt deposits are the foundation of a lucrative industry in an area known primarily for its warm waters and lovely beaches.

Minor folds in the earth and erosion create ridges and valleys which determine the coast's outline. Such ridges form the headlands at Pugwash and Wallace and nearly enclose Malagash Point and Amet Sound.

Lakes are uncommon on this coastal plain, and, where they occur, are elongated and shallow. West of Pictou, progressively older rocks are exposed and are more resistant, forming a hilly, upland projection. From Merigomish to McArras Brook the Northumberland Plain continues as a rolling coastal lowland.

The most common trees in this region are black spruce, jack pine, white spruce, red spruce and red maple, interspersed with occasional hemlock and white pine. Larch and black spruce occur in the extensive boggy areas. Beech and sugar maple are found on a few slopes near larger streams. Much of the area is farmed and old fields generally recolonize in alders followed by white spruce.

Winds from the Northumberland Strait have a strong influence on the trees growth patterns. They bend with the wind and are stunted in growth, a phenomenon known as *krummholz*. Extensive salt marshes and eelgrass beds border tidal bays.

This is an excellent area for muskrat, mink, and raccoon, and provides

Windsurfing off Brule Beach.

average habitat for Red Fox. Important waterfowl breeding and migratory staging areas are found along the coast because of the extensive intertidal areas formed by the very shallow slope of the sea bottom. Around Fox Harbour, Wallace Harbour, Tatamagouche Bay, Brule Harbour and John Bay, large numbers of ducks and geese congregate in late March and early April, and again in September until ice forms in December. Other migratory areas include Coldspring Head and the mouth of the Shinimicas River; Pugwash Harbour and River Philip; Caribou Harbour; Pictou Harbour, East River, Middle River, and West River; Little Harbour and Merigomish Harbour. Bald Eagle and Osprey breeding habitat occurs here, and Piping Plover breeding sites are found on some of the larger sand beaches.

A panoramic view of the Northumberland Strait is offered just north of Amherst. The first village along the shore is Tidnish, a Micmac word meaning "a paddle." This was the site for the Northumberland terminus of the Chignecto Ship Railway Project, which was to convey schooners and boats across land to the head of the Bay of Fundy. It started in 1890 but was later abandoned due to a lack of funds. Today, remains of the old roadbed and masonry are still visible and a stone culvert can be seen at the Riverside Trailer Court at Tidnish Bridge. A collection of photographs are on display at the Tidnish Tourist Bureau. From Tidnish Dock, a left turn leads to Tidnish Dock Provincial Park, a day-use area that was once the northern terminus of the Railway. Wooden pilings from the wharf are still visible. There is a small beach below the park grounds.

Northport is a mixed farming and fishing community located at the mouth of the Shinimicas River. There is a lobster pound near the bridge. Northport Beach Park is a provincial day-use park on the Northumberland Strait with a narrow, sandy beach. Clamming is a popular activity, particularly at low tide in the spring. Nearby is Heather Beach Provincial Park, a popular swimming spot.

Shinimicas Bridge has cat-tail ditches and brooks, habitat for some molluscs and fish including the Brook Stickleback, a rare species in Nova Scotia. Shinimicas Provincial Park provides an attractive site for picnicking on the bank of the Shinimicas River.

Port Howe is a fishing community on the west bank of the River Philip where the river empties into Pugwash Bay. A lobster pound is located here to hold Northumberland's May and June catch, and numerous other lobster pounds, where lobster may be purchased, are found along this shore. The lobster fishermen set and haul traps early in the morning, and the boats generally return to shore by early afternoon.

On the other side of the bridge is Port Philip on the River Philip, a tidal river with good trout and salmon fishing and opportunities for water sports and boating. There is a boat launch at the wharf in Port Philip and several seafood restaurants are nearby.

Northumberland Shore

Pugwash is a shipping, fishing, and mining centre located on an excellent harbour at the mouth of the Pugwash River. A waterfront park and nearby beach make the town a popular stop. Pugwash Harbour accommodates fishing boats, lumber freighters, and ships loading raw salt from the salt mine and evaporation plant, which has been in operation since 1956. Pugwash celebrates its Scottish heritage each July 1st by staging the Gathering of the Clans.

The Gulf Shore Road leads southward along the coast and is the location of Smith Point, one of several points of land that typify the area. On this route there is a provincial day-use park with picnic facilities and an excellent sand beach with warm water at MacLeans Point. There are also small roadside beaches around Fox Harbour and Wallace Bay. The upper reaches of Wallace Bay are maintained by the Canadian Wildlife Service as a bird sanctuary, and access to the wetlands is limited.

Wallace is another fishing community and has a major sandstone quarry. Many buildings in Canada and the United States, including the Parliament Buildings in Ottawa and Province House in Halifax, are made from Wallace sandstone. Now primarily a fishing, farming, and lumbering centre, Wallace has a busy public wharf. Lobsters, oysters, and quahogs may be purchased in season and there is a boat-building shop in town. Just on the outskirts of town is the Wallace Harbour lighthouse. Wallace Harbour is a designated National Wildlife Area.

A coastal highway can be taken around the Malagash peninsula where salt mines were once located. Today, a miners' cemetery is the only evidence of past activity, which lasted from 1918 to 1956.

Rushton's Beach Provincial Park near Brule has a salt marsh behind the beach which is ideal for bird-watching.

Tatamagouche, a farming and fishing town situated at the mouth of the French and Waugh Rivers, where they empty into Tatamagouche Bay, derives its name from a Micmac word meaning "meeting place of the waters." This bay is habitat for quahogs, dwarf surf clams and other warm water molluscs and crustaceans which have been isolated from southern populations for several thousands of years.

Once an Acadian settlement, Tatamagouche now houses the Sunrise Trail Museum, with exhibits on Micmac and Acadian culture and nineteenth-century agriculture, shipbuilding, and lifestyles. The community holds a festival from late June to early July and lobster suppers take place in July and August. Deep-sea fishing charters are available from the town.

At Bayhead, west of Tatamagouche, you can fish for striped bass, mackerel, cod, and flounder. Windsurfing is popular on the bay.

River John is a fishing village on the River John at the head of John Bay. Lobster is the primary catch and can be purchased at the famous suppers here

Northumberland Shore

Melmerby Beach offers warm waters for ocean swimming and miles of sand for hiking.

in May, June, and July. There are several fine beaches, a wharf, and a lobster pound on the Cape John Road on the outskirts of the village.

Toney River is a fishing village situated on the Toney River where it empties into Northumberland Strait. From the highway, the coast of Prince Edward Island can be seen 24 km (15 mi.) away. Here, fishermen gather Irish moss which can be seen drying on the side of the road. There is a seaweed reduction plant here where moss is processed into coagulants.

Just past Toney River, a left turn on the shore road leads along the coast to Caribou River and Caribou Island. Just before Caribou Island is a provincial park with a fine sand beach at water's edge. This road can be followed all the way around Caribou Harbour to the town of Pictou.

Ferries at Caribou provide frequent daily service to Wood Islands, P.E.I. throughout the year with the exception of the winter months, when the Northumberland Strait is ice-bound. A large fish cannery and provincial recreation park are located near the ferry terminal.

Near the causeway crossing Pictou Harbour, a breeding colony of Double-crested Cormorants is established on the remains of an old pier.

Abercrombie, a small Pictou Harbour village at the mouth of the East River with a superb view, was marked on an early French map as the site of a large Micmac village and many artifacts have been uncovered here.

Pictou is one of the largest communities on the Northumberland Shore and is called "the birthplace of New Scotland" because it was here that Nova Scotia's first Scottish Highlanders landed. Pictou has a marina, a fisheries museum, and a summer Lobster Carnival in early July, celebrated since 1934.

Nesting cormorants.

Northumberland Shore

Abercrombie Wildlife Management Area with its seabird colonies, waterfowl, and Bald Eagles, is near here.

Powells Point Provincial Park on the coast from New Glasgow has the warmest salt water in Nova Scotia. Nearby Melmerby Beach Provincial Park contains a wide variety of coastal habitats typical of the Northumberland Shore: a large sand beach, salt marshes, coastal spruce forest, and sandspits.

Just along the coast is the village of Merigomish which takes its name from the Micmac word for "place of merrymaking." The Micmac gathered here for summer sports that included running, highjumps, and wrestling.

Just below Lower Barney's River, a left turn leads to Merigomish Island, where there is a large sandy beach with large timbers embedded in the sand to prevent erosion.

2.1.1   Activities: Pugwash
Tour a Coastal Town, Take a Boat Ride

The Northumberland Shore has a peaceful quality lying as it does in the shelter of Prince Edward Island. Pugwash, on the shore's northwestern side, used to be the location of the world famous Thinkers' Conferences, where intellectuals and world leaders would gather to discuss world problems. The organizer, native son and American industrialist Cyrus W. Eaton, loved the area and returned every summer bringing international figures with him.

To get to Pugwash, take Route 366 to Tidnish from Amherst, and at Port Howe, take Route 6 to Pugwash, a distance of approximately 50 km (31 mi.).

Spend the morning walking the town and visiting the craft store, which features pewter and many local crafts. Include in your walk a pass by the Pugwash salt mine, where the largest deposit in Canada and some of the purest salt in the world is mined and refined.

If the weather is nice, take a drive out to Heather Beach where you'll find quahogs (large clams) and razor clams in the mud at low tide. To get to Heather Beach, backtrack on Route 6 toward Amherst, then exit right onto Route 366, a total of approximately 12 km (7.5 mi.).

After your afternoon on the beach, return to Pugwash and a drive to Pugwash Point across the harbour (turn right toward the coast and go approximately 5 km (3 mi.).

For those interested in a sail on a converted lobster boat, a boat tour leaves from near Pugwash. Veteran fisherman Howard Ferdinand will explain the history of the fishing industry in the area as you cruise along. To find the dock, take Route 6 west of Pugwash at Brickyard Marina. It's a two and a half hour tour leaving daily. Telephone 902-243-2382 for information.

Map: Amherst to Pugwash

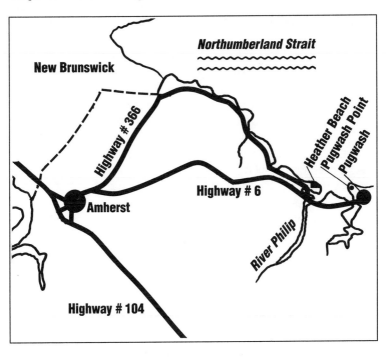

Activities: Malagash
Cycle and Sip Tour

You begin your cycling tour of the Malagash peninsula at Wallace, on Route 6, a picturesque lobster-fishery village. This trip takes you through countryside where a huge salt deposit was discovered in 1927 ("Nine Square Miles of Pure Rock Salt Under Green Fields of Malagash," the headline read). You'll travel along the placid shores of the Northumberland Strait, over bulrush and salt marshes, and past vineyards of the developing wine industry in the area. The lobster (in season May and June) here is among the best in Nova Scotia and wine tasters have awarded top marks to some of the local wines. Stop for a lobster feed, a sip of wine, and a swim along the shore.

This tour of approximately 49 km (30.4 mi.) over flat to slightly rolling terrain, will take the novice cyclist five to six hours to complete including two hours for a lunch break and swim.

Buy a lobster, cooked or live, from the wharf in Wallace up to July 1 and again after August 10, or live at the store on the main street all summer long. The general store sells first rate home baking to complete your meal.

Northumberland Shore

It's about 3 km (1.9 mi.) to the first paved road where you turn left to the Malagash Peninsula. Continue for 8 km (5 mi.) until you see the wine keg sign which will direct you to the winery. Here you can sample the wines before buying.

From here, turn right to continue along the coast for 5 km (3 mi.) past Malagash Mine. In 1927, a local farmer began to wonder why his well water tasted salty and then discovered it was sitting on a huge salt vein, which, along with coal and gypsum, is one of the valuable mineral deposits in the region. Turn left at the T and go 6 km (3.7 mi.) to the left turn which will take you to the end of the Malagash Point Road. There are accessible beaches 1 or 2 km (1.2 mi.) up the road. From here, backtrack and continue straight along a road that hugs the coast for most of its 16 km (9.9 mi.). You'll pass through a grove of bulrushes and a salt marsh, important coastal incubators for microscopic marine life.

After the coastal ride past Malagash, you'll connect to Route 6 where you'll turn right for an 8 km (5 mi.) ride back to Wallace.

2.1.4   Map: Wallace to Malagash Point

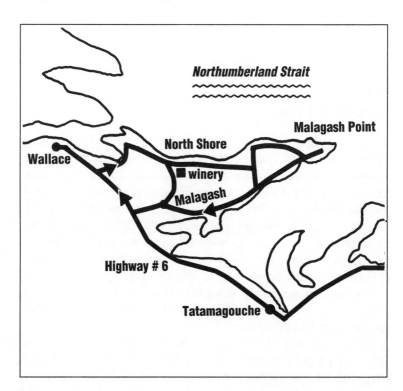

Area: McArras Brook to Arisaig — Pictou Valleys   2.2

From the slow rhythm of the Northumberland, travelling southeastward, we enter the eastern portion of the Pictou Valley district around McArras Brook. This hilly area extends westwards between the Cobequid Hills and the Pictou–Antigonish Highlands and is predominantly composed of sandstone and siltstone with minor gypsum and anhydrite deposits. Because these rocks are more resistant than others, the elevations have been maintained, despite the streams which dissect the area.

Part of the East River north of Sunnybrae is a fossil valley that became filled with soil deposits but is gradually being re-exposed. In the central part of the Pictou Valleys is the Pictou Coalfield. This basin, developed from downfaulting, was a sedimentary sink, later providing a suitable environment for coal seams to develop. The seams underly an area of about 5 km by 10 km (3 mi. by 10 mi.) beneath New Glasgow, Stellarton, and Trenton. Eleven of the 45 seams have been mined. The coal seams were formed in a period when the earth's plates were unstable, and periods of plant growth alternated with inundations by muds.

Soils in this district are productive and much of the area is farmed. White spruce and balsam fir grow on old fields and pastures. Sugar maple, yellow birch, and beech grow on slopes, with some hardwoods and aspen.

Arisaig village was settled in 1791 by Catholic Highlanders. A plaque near the church commemorates their arrival. A provincial park located here has picnic facilities, a walking trail, and a boardwalk to the beach. The fossils in sedimentary rock along this shore are of particular interest.

Activities: Arisaig   2.2.1
Walking Among Fossils

The constantly crumbling Arisaig cliffs are filled with fossils. As you walk along the beach, eroding layers of shale will reveal well-preserved specimens of the past.

From Sutherland's River east of New Glasgow, pick up Route 245 which will take you along the coast to Arisaig. Turn left at the church and go down the Arisaig Wharf Road where you can park, and purchase cooked lobster in season.

Turning west, walk past a second, unused wharf, along the beach past the government picnic ground (which you'll return to for your lunch), cross McDougall's Brook (or Arisaig Brook as it's designated on some maps), and search for fossils in the cliffs that are to your left. Check tide tables before going.

Northumberland Shore

The fossils you collect can be taken to the Nova Scotia Museum in Halifax for identification.

When you've had your fill of exploring the layers of time, backtrack across the brook and take the footpath along the boardwalk up to the picnic grounds for lunch. Then hike back along the highway to Arisaig Wharf Road to join up with your car or bicycle.

2.2.2　Map: Arisaig Point and McDougall's Brook

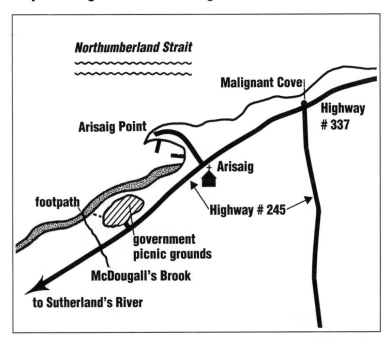

2.3　Area: Malignant Cove to Lakevale — Antigonish Uplands

North of the town of Antigonish is an area called the "Antigonish Upland," featuring varying types of rock, some resistant, others easily eroded, and still others volcanic. These areas, cut by faults and elevated and dissected by streams, represent a transitional zone between the coastal lowland and the uplands to the west and south. This area provides mainly forested habitats, with cliffs along St. George's Bay.

A scenic drive, known as the "Mini Cabot Trail" (in reference to the trail over the Cape Breton Highlands) winds from Malignant Cove to the tip of Cape George. It follows the shore of St. George's Bay (which has excellent beaches) and passes through the communities of Ballantyne Cove, Cape George, Lakevale, Morristown, Crystal Cliffs, and Antigonish Harbour. The lighthouse at Ballantyne's Cove, first built in 1895, is situated 304.8 m (1000 ft) above St. George's Bay. From this vantage point on a clear day you can see Prince Edward and Cape Breton Islands.

Activities: Cape George   2.3.1
Hike the Headland (2 days)

This trip will take you through unspoiled countryside and deciduous forest. The ocean is visible from a lighthouse-topped hill and the tips of both Prince Edward Island and Cape Breton can be viewed from Cape George Point.

Head east from Arisaig and park at the turn-off to Cape George at Malignant Cove. Your first day is the longer one, a hike of approximately 37 km (22.9 mi.). Bring drinks and snacks with you as the only restaurant is at Livingstone's Cove 13 km (8 mi.). (If you are coming from Antigonish, the health food store stocks lots of high energy bars, juices, and trail mixes). Phone ahead for reservations at the cottages in Cribbons Point. A local tourist bureau can provide particulars.

Once you get to Livingstone's Cove, the forests of the first 13 km (8 mi.) opens to a more rolling, coastal hill country. You're climbing consistently after this until you reach Cape George Point where you'll round the point and begin a descent at 18 km (11.1 mi.). At 21 km (13 mi.) you'll take the lighthouse road where you can have a fabulous lunch of lobster. If you're here in late June, the hill will be covered with wild strawberries.

The view here is spectacular. To your left the flattish coast of Prince Edward Island can be seen. Off in the distance to your right are the higher ranges of the Cape Breton Highlands.

If you wish to leave lunch until later, you can hike to Ballantyne's Cove, 2 km (1.2 mi.) up the road, where fish and chips is available.

The coast is in view until before Lakevale. At 39 km (24.2 mi.), a road on the left leads to the cottages about 2 km (1.2 mi.) away where rest and relaxation awaits you after a long day's effort.

Your second day is a lot shorter 24 km (14.4 mi.) so you can spend the early morning on the beach sunning and swimming. Around noon, head out to the highway where you'll backtrack (turn right Route 337 north) and just before you cross the bridge, at the 4 km (2.5 mi.) mark, turn left to Fairmont. At the Y in the the road, bear right to Big Marsh. This is a pretty, secondary road through mixed forest and cleared farmland. Notice the red sand that makes up this terrain. Take another right and at the Y in the road, bear right to Big Marsh or continue on, connecting with Route 245 west, to Malignant Cove.

Northumberland Shore

2.3.2   Map: Malignant Cove, Cape George, Cribbons Point

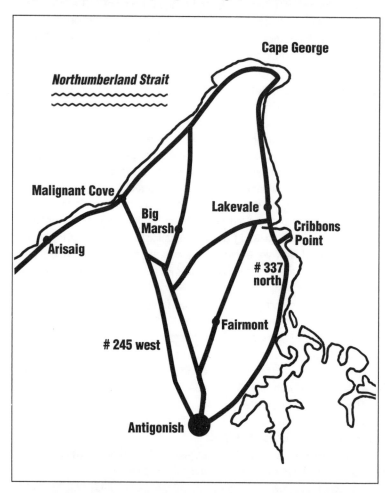

2.4   Area: Antigonish to Havre Boucher — St. George's Bay

This eastern section of the Northumberland Plain, a low-lying plain of fine red sandstones, runs along the coast of St. George's Bay from Antigonish Harbour to the Canso Causeway which connects Cape Breton Island to the mainland. Around St. George's Bay, elevations rarely exceed 48.8 m (160 ft). Fine red and grey/brown sandstones and siltstones predominate with a faulted block of evaporites exposed east of Antigonish. On the south side of St. George's Bay several harbours have been created from drowned river valleys cut into Carboniferous rocks—Pomquet, Tracadie, and Havre Boucher. At Crystal

Cliffs to the north, a 76.2 m (250 ft) high cliff with bands of white and pink gypsum faces the bay.

The coast can be reached from Antigonish travelling to Pomquet, which was settled in 1761 by Acadians from the port of St. Malo, France. Pomquet beach has a graduated sand dune system which is worth visiting. Swimming is enjoyable since water temperatures are a relatively warm 15-20 °C (65-70 °F), typical of most beaches in the area.

Bayfield, a village named in honour of Admiral Bayfield, who surveyed the Gulf of St. Lawrence before 1854, features a busy wharf, a sandy beach, an offshore lighthouse, and on Pomquet Island, a nesting ground for seagulls.

Tracadie, originally inhabited by Acadians, has mixed farming, lumbering, and lobster fishing (during the spring months). Few would argue that there's anything sweeter or more succulent than a Northumberland Shore lobster. Monastery offers sea-trout fishing on the Tracadie River.

Havre Boucher further along the coast, operates tuna charters; boats are available for hire, and lobster is available for sale during May and June.

Auld Cove is a fishing village on the Strait of Canso. This area of St. George's Bay has recently been the locale for tuna sport fishing, prompted by the late fall run of giant Bluefin Tuna that congregate north of the Causeway to feed on mackerel.

This is the entrance of Cape Breton Island and the Canso Causeway, which, at 66 m (217 ft), is the deepest causeway in the world.

Inland channels to the sea offer a rich kayaking experience.

Northumberland Shore

2.4.1   Activities: Havre Boucher
Tail the Tuna on a Charter Boat

At Havre Boucher wharf, a fleet of white longliners and Cape Island boats, trimmed with various hues and sporting the names of loved ones, bob in the brisk ocean wind. The fishing grounds out of this wharf offer one of the best chances left in Nova Scotia to catch a Bluefin Tuna. The season begins in August and ends in October with September being the best month. A full day on a tuna charter is $250.00, but a group charter would cut down individual expenses and present a unique opportunity.

Your day begins in Antigonish where you'll take Route 104 toward Cape Breton. Turn off at exit 37 and drive to Monastery where you can angle fish for sea trout in the Tracadie River. If you're looking for spiritual solace, inquire about retreat opportunities at the Augustinian Monastery here.

Continue to Havre Boucher where you'll find your charter boat at the end of Government Wharf Road. Friendly French sailors will be your guides for a day of unforgettable deep-sea fishing for tuna. Wear warm clothes, sunglasses, sun block, and pack a lunch.

2.4.2   Map: Antigonish to Havre Boucher

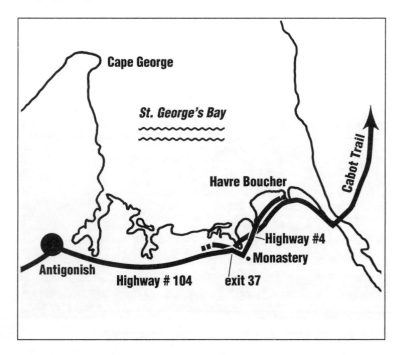

Region: Cape Breton Island Coast

Ceilidh, Fleur-de-lis and Cabot Trails

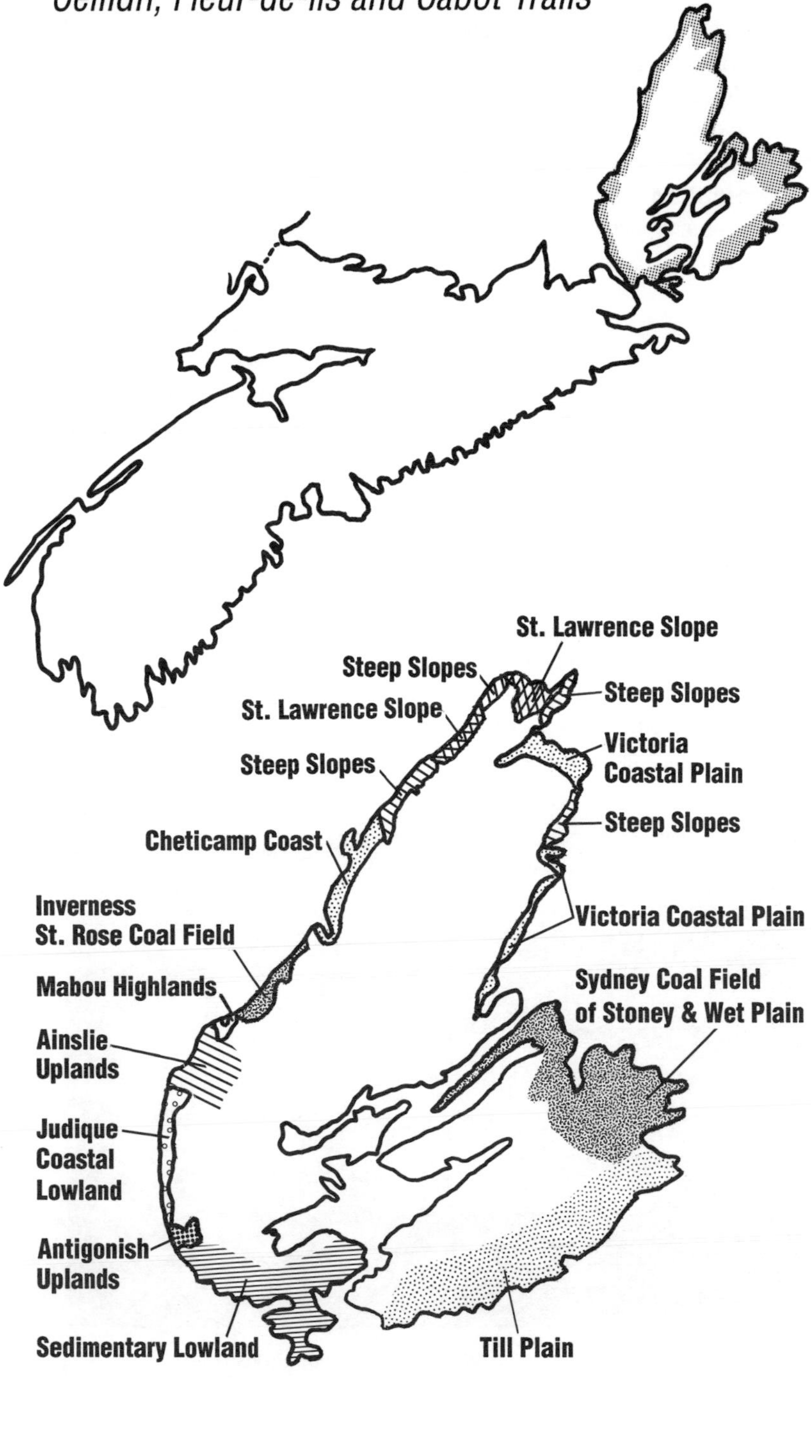
St. Lawrence Slope
Steep Slopes
St. Lawrence Slope
Steep Slopes
Steep Slopes
Victoria Coastal Plain
Steep Slopes
Cheticamp Coast
Inverness St. Rose Coal Field
Victoria Coastal Plain
Mabou Highlands
Sydney Coal Field of Stoney & Wet Plain
Ainslie Uplands
Judique Coastal Lowland
Antigonish Uplands
Sedimentary Lowland
Till Plain

Writers and poets have all searched for metaphors to describe the magic of Cape Breton Island. It has been called "Island of Islands," "The Jewel in the Pig's Snout," "A Tin Can Tied to a Dog's Tail," "A Rock in the Stream," and "Home of Our Hearts," among other imaginative descriptions.

Cape Breton is a land mass formed by glacial activity, the shifting of continents, and the ebb and flow of tides. It contains lowlands, uplands, slopes, coal fields, and plains, but its culture is inextricably tied to the sea. Coal features in the lives of many Cape Bretoners and a rich mining culture keeps its history alive.

Cape Breton Island has no less than twelve distinctive theme regions which include three trails: the "Ceilidh Trail," the "Fleur-de-Lis Trail," and the "Cabot Trail." It is a place to hike, climb or cycle, whale-watch, bird-watch, or swim or sail. The coastal scenery is beautiful anywhere in Cape Breton and you are never more than fifteen miles from the sea.

The Micmac were the first Cape Breton sailors; they built large boats from bark and hides. Acadians developed the "chaloupe" (sometimes called "shallop,") a smaller sailing vessel. The schooner made its debut as a seaworthy fishing vessel in the 1700s and is still a popular design but is now used for sailing and racing.

Today, container ships travel up the Strait of Canso carrying oil, coal, and steel. Fishermen use vessels equipped with hydraulic machinery and electronic detection systems while pleasure boaters canoe, kayak, or sail wood and fibreglass boats along the Island's craggy coast.

Cape Breton
Island Coast

The Cape Breton coastline beckons the more adventurous bikers.

Area: Canso Causeway to Creignish — Antigonish Uplands

Cape Breton beckons us across "The causeway," and we become islanders, if only temporarily. The small land mass on the left has geological ties to the mainland. This area is part of the Lakevale district of the Antigonish Uplands, which are cut by faults and slightly elevated, and represents a transitional zone between the coastal lowland and the uplands to the west and south. Softwoods are prevalent here. This small section leads into the Judique Coastal Lowland.

Area: Creignish to Judique — Judique Coastal Lowland

The Judique coastal lowland forms a narrow band along the eastern side of St. Georges Bay and is a continuation of the Northumberland Plain region. Geologists believe that the entire Bay area was once composed of the same material that is now only exposed at the edges. There is also evidence that the Bay may have been carved out by an ancestral river flowing from the Scotian Shelf through the Strait of Canso.

Softwoods are dominant but sugar maple also occurs. Many of the old fields are regenerating in white spruce and balsam fir. Black spruce and larch are found in wetter areas.

Judique (a name of possible French origin) was founded in 1776 by families who migrated from the Hebrides in Scotland. Local legends recount feats of Scottish strong men and their zest for life. Their dancing skills are immortalized in "Judique-on-the-Floor Days" held every summer.

There is a beach in the community and deep-sea fishing expeditions leave from the Judique North wharf during the summer months. At Little Judique Harbour fresh fish and lobster may be purchased in season. Lobsters are caught along the bay shore in May and June only.

Boat tours and charters are available at Port Hood, a large fishing port.

Activities: Judique North Dangle a Line in the Deep

To get to Pig Cove Wharf, take Route 19 at the causeway toward Inverness and continue 3.5 km (2 mi.) past Judique, before leaving the main highway for a drive along Shore Road with its brooks, ponds, and fishing wharves. You will cross Judique Intervale Brook and MacKay's Pond before taking a road on the

Cape Breton Island Coast

left which leads to MacKay's Wharf, the first of the three wharves on this road. You can buy lobsters in May and June.

Backtrack to Shore Road and continue north 6.5 km (4 mi.) until you see a sign to Pig Cove Wharf. Watch for eagles on this stretch of road, especially in the late afternoon, and for Great Blue Herons, a tall bluish-grey bird. Inquire about fishing charters on the wharves here, or simply cast your line off the wharf to catch pollack or cod. After a fishing experience to remember, continue on to Little Judique Harbour and reconnect there with Route 19.

3.2.2   **Map: Port Hastings to Little Judique Harbour**

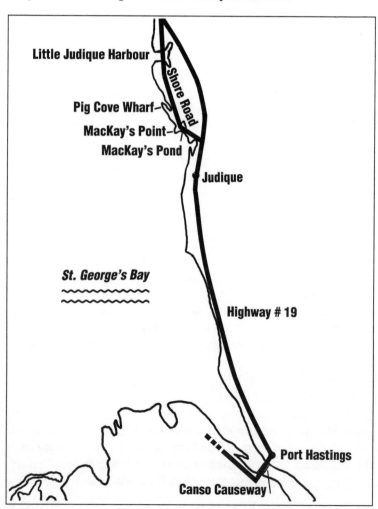

Little Judique Harbour

Shore Road

Pig Cove Wharf

MacKay's Point

MacKay's Pond

Judique

St. George's Bay

Highway # 19

Port Hastings

Canso Causeway

Cape Breton
Island Coast

Area: Mabou Harbour Mouth — Ainslie Uplands   3.3

Mabou, a small island village, is the first upland area on our travels.

The Mabou area, covering a large expanse from St. George's Bay to Lake Ainslie, includes West Mabou Harbour, Mabou Mines, and Mabou. This is a hilly, fairly rugged region of folds, erosion, faults, and volcanic rock. Glacial deposits are transported from the Cape Breton Highlands by fast running streams, and coarse glacial gravels are evident on the lower slopes of the Mabou Hills.

West Mabou Beach is one of the most popular recreation spots in the vicinity and the coastal scenery from its vantage point is some of the finest on the island.

As the highest and one of the most northerly districts in the Carboniferous Lowlands Region, the Ainslie Uplands are part of the maple/yellow birch/fir zone, representative of many of the highlands in Nova Scotia.

Activities: Sight Point   3.3.1
View the Scenery on a Coastal Beach Walk

The first highlands look deceptively low. These are the Mabou Highlands, peaks of up to 304 m (1000 ft), which protect the surrounding communities from the winds off the Gulf of St. Lawrence. There is a great hiking trail here that winds in a loop around the base of a 274 m (900 ft) mountain which begins and ends at Mabou Mines. The approximately 21 km (13 mi.) hike calls for a pack sack of beverages, nutritious foods, and snacks for fuel, plus good hiking shoes. Allow four hours for the walk, including stops.

To get to Sight Point, take Route 19 to Mabou, and at the intersection of Routes 19 and 252 turn left toward Mabou Harbour Mouth. Go approximately 5 km (3 mi.) and turn right toward Mabou Mines. Travel approximately 4.5 km (2.8 mi.) and park your car along the shoulder of the road near the Sight Point sign. Then hike the rolling, tree-lined dirt road that dips and curls along woodland countryside and rugged coast.

The 9.5 km (5.9 mi.) hike to Sight Point follows a straight course from MacDonald's Glen approximately 2.5 km (1.6 mi.). There is a loop around Cape Mabou to MacKinnon's Brook 3 km (1.9 mi.) and on to Sight Point 4 km (2.5 mi.), then inland back to MacDonald's Glen 9 km (5.6 mi.) and back to Mabou Mines 2.5 km (1.6 mi.). You will want to stop often to take advantage of the varied and impressive scenery.

End your day with a drive to West Mabou Beach. From MacDonald's Glen, Return to Mabou along Route 252, turning right onto Route 19 for 2 km (1.2 mi.) before taking the first right at the sign to "West Mabou Harbour," a drive of

Cape Breton
Island Coast

approximately 5 km (3.1 mi.). West Mabou Beach, one of the area's most popular beaches, is just past West Mabou Harbour. It provides a wonderful view of the Northumberland Strait and Prince Edward Island.

3.3.2 Map: Colindale to Sight Point

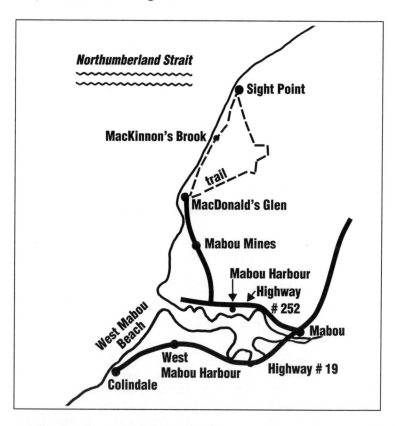

3.4   Area: Mabou — Mabou Highlands

Near McKinnon Brook is a coastal fragment of the Mabou Highlands. Broad Cove, a little further north, exhibits fine sandy deposits on its banks, ascending to over 152.4 m (500 ft) above sea level.

Protected from the winds off the Gulf of St. Lawrence, tolerant hardwoods dominate the upland plateau in this area, with sugar maple, yellow birch and beech being the main species. White spruce and balsam fir are found on coastal sites, while balsam fir, spruce and hemlock form softwood stands or mixed wood stands with red maple and birch on the lower slopes.

Activities: Mabou   3.4.1
Sea Kayak Mabou to Port Hood Island (4 days)

A trip to the Highlands is even more enjoyable when viewing the rugged coastal scenery from the deck of a boat. Whatever type of boat you prefer—sail, motor yacht, Cape Islander, or kayak—can be experienced in Cape Breton.

While you're in the Mabou area, take the opportunity to try kayaking—a perfect place for beginners and veterans alike. You can paddle from the inland coastal harbour of Mabou to the outer coastal island of Port Hood. The full journey is some 20 km (12.4 mi.) of persistent paddling along the scenic Mabou River down to the ocean, but you can choose your own distance.

The contrast in scenery is exciting; warm waters and fine sandy beaches are ringed by rugged pine-clad hills. Port Hood Island has fascinating rock formations and bird colonies. Nearby is uninhabited Henry Island "in the spirit of Robinson Crusoe, a place to linger and reflect…" as the kayaking brochure describes it.

Kayak (or cycling) equipment can be rented from the local kayaking outfitters, Kayak Cape Breton, who schedule a variety of tours, including a four-day kayak adventure in late June (telephone 902-535-3060). There are also "custom-designed" programs for individuals and groups.

Enjoying the rugged coastline of Cape Breton in a sea kayak.

Cape Breton
Island Coast

53

3.4.2   Map: Mabou Harbour to Henry Island

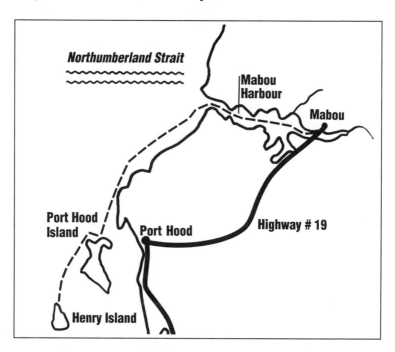

3.5   Area: Inverness to Grand Etang —
Inverness St. Rose Coalfield

Further along the Ceilidh Trail is a narrow fringe of Carboniferous strata called the Coastal Fringe. This forms a flat area at the base of the steep shoulder of volcanic rock which flanks the Highlands. From Inverness northwards towards Margaree Harbour a hilly, faulted narrow belt forms a small basin containing coal seams. Coal has been mined here, but the seams dip steeply out under the Northumberland Strait so much of the coal deposit is inaccessible.

The vegetation is influenced by the prevailing westerly winds off the Gulf of St. Lawrence. White spruce is the most common species, but tolerant hardwoods are found on the better drained and more sheltered sites. Black spruce and larch grow in wet, depressioned areas. Elsewhere, a mixed forest of spruce, fir and pine, with maple and birch, is widespread. Marsh marigolds can be found in wet places.

Margaree Island provides breeding habitat for several species of sea birds, including Black Guillemots.

At Inverness, the largest town on the Ceilidh Trail, there is a supervised

Cape Breton
Island Coast

54

beach, where windsurfing is a popular sport. The townscape is dotted with company houses built for miners, a reminder of the days when Inverness was a major mining town.

Activities: Inverness
Windsurf the Waves, Catch a Salmon

Inverness, north of Mabou on Route 19, once a mining town, now a fishing port, is blessed with a magnificent beach and warm waters from the gulf stream. Board sailing or windsurfing are popular here and a centre for rental, instruction, and camps is at your disposal. If you've never tried board sailing, Inverness is the place to learn. Four-hour classes introduce you to the art and science of controlling a sail-mantled surfboard.

After a day on the beach trying your hand (and legs) on the board, visit the miners' museum to learn about the history of coal mining in this area. The inaccessibility of the coal illustrates the limits of man's ingenuity in finding safe methods for extracting natural resources, even in this technological age. Inverness is a prime example of a community's ability to change its economic base by utilizing its resources in a new way.

After a day in Inverness, continue up Route 19 to Dunvegan where a right

Salmon fishing on the Margaree River.

Cape Breton
Island Coast

turn inland to Southwest Margaree, then left to Northeast Margaree, will take you into salmon fishing country, among the best in the world. There are regulations governing fishing in the area (licenses, restricted areas, legal limit, bait, etc.) and any local store or garage will give you information and sell you a license. Canoes for the Margaree River are available for rental from the Duck Cove Inn in Margaree. You need to have your own fishing tackle, but the thrill of salmon fishing is on the house.

3.5.2   Map: Inverness Beach

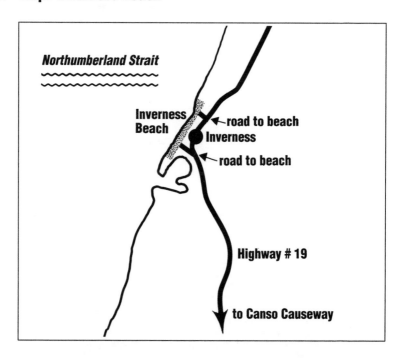

3.6   Area: Grand Etang to Cheticamp — Cheticamp Coast

The town of Cheticamp marks the beginning of the Cape Breton Highlands National Park, but geologically it is connected to the adjacent southern region. The coastal fringe continues beyond Margaree Harbour in a thin strip of rock overlain by red sandstone, siltstones, and greyish sandstones, forming a narrow coastal plain. The overlying rock forms a valley at the base of the highland slope where gypsum occurs. Near Cheticamp, where the plain broadens, extensive gypsum deposits have been mined down to the underlying rock.

Cheticamp has beaches, a public wharf, wonderful seafood restaurants featuring Acadian cuisine, and other recreational facilities.

Descendants of the original Acadians first landed at Cheticamp Island in 1755 but soon moved inland to settle on the mountain plateau. They began as inland farmers, but they later became fishermen, building chaloupes and harvesting the abundance of the sea. A strong craft tradition of rug hooking and tapestries has made the craftspeople of Cheticamp world famous.

Cheticamp Island is composed of red sandstone and is eroding rapidly. It is connected to the mainland by a long sand and gravel bar. Just to the north, coastal erosion has reduced a deposit of red sandstone to stacks which lie at the mouth of Trout Brook. The sandstone generally forms low cliffs along the shore.

Cheticamp Island has a public beach with tennis courts. On the northern tip of the island, at Enragee Point, is a picturesque lighthouse. During the summer months, daily boat trips leave Cheticamp, offering the chance to do some whale-watching.

North of Cheticamp Village is a formation of glacial outwash material. A bar has formed across the mouth of the Cheticamp River and an esker projects out to the bar dividing the lagoon into two ponds.

At Chimney Corner thin coal seams in the sandstone and siltstone can be seen along the shore.

Margaree Harbour is a picturesque fishing village at the mouth of the Margaree River. The 39-metre schooner *Marion Elizabeth* is docked in the harbour. Built in 1918 by the same Lunenburg firm that built the *Bluenose,* the *Marion Elizabeth* has been restored to house a restaurant and museum. There are excellent beaches at Margaree Harbour, nearby Whale Cove, Chimney Corner, and Belle Cote.

Grand Etang ("big pond") is a fishing community situated snugly around a landlocked harbour.

Petit Etang, a proposed provincial ecological site, has a marsh with several uncommon plants. There is also a four-hour hiking trail that takes you to the top of the local highlands for a panoramic view of the area.

The entrance to the Cape Breton Highlands National Park is 4.8 km (3 mi.) from Cheticamp on the Cabot Trail near Petit Etang. The park is approximately 958 sq. km (370 sq. mi.) in area, lying between the Gulf of St. Lawrence and the Atlantic Ocean. It forms part of a great tableland that rises precipitously in many places from sea level to a height of 538 m (1,750 ft).

Cape Breton
Island Coast

3.6.1   Activities: Cheticamp
Hike in the Morning, Whale-Watch in the Afternoon

Cheticamp, the largest Acadian community in Nova Scotia, is at the entrance to the Cape Breton Highlands National Park where your activities will centre on hiking. Before you embark on some of the most fantastic coastal and wilderness hiking in North America, immerse yourself in Acadian culture by exploring the town. Begin your day walking the town's Main Street, shopping for Acadian crafts, and having breakfast at one of the restaurants. (Book a whale-watching charter at the wharf before you put on your hiking boots.)

Your hike begins at Belle Marche (just behind Cheticamp) and continues inland along a trail around Aucoin Brook. To get to Belle Marche turn right at the Cheticamp Post Office and go 2 km (1.2 mi.) before turning right for 1 km (.6 mi.) onto Plantain Road. A short ride from there is the trail's entrance that leads up the mountain and around Aucoin Brook, a loop of approximately 14 km (8.7 mi.) that leads back to the highway. It is another 2.5 km (1.6 mi.) back to your vehicle. Make sure to take food, water, insect repellant, and wear comfortable hiking shoes as this trail is uphill at least half of the way.

A more structured hike in this area begins at the entrance to the National Park. Called the Acadian Trail, this two-hour hike takes you to the top of the local highlands and offers a panoramic view of the Cheticamp area.

Whichever hike you choose, you will want to satisfy your appetite before setting out for your whale-watching charter. This is an excellent whale-watching area and you can look forward to sightings of seis, minkes, pilots, finbacks, humpbacks, and maybe even a rare sighting of the now almost extinct blue whale, the largest animal in existence. Whale-watching tours also offer superb bird-watching opportunities and some skippers will make detours specifically for this purpose.

Binoculars, camera, warm clothing, sun lotion, and snack food are standard equipment on these trips.

Cape Breton
Island Coast

The Pleasant Bay area offers hiking and biking adventures for novices and enthusiasts.

Map: Cheticamp

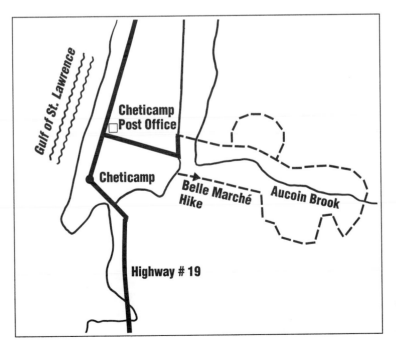

Cape Breton
Island Coast

3.6.3   **Map: Rue des Habitations Neuves**

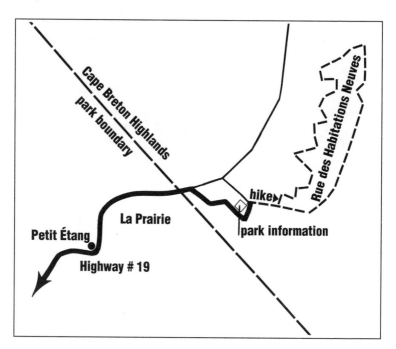

3.7   Area: Pleasant Bay to Lowland Cove — St. Lawrence Slope

To hike, canoe, or cycle through the Cape Breton Highlands Park provides the opportunity to experience real solitude. Trails lead along windswept ridges with breathtaking views, while others descend into coastal valleys or follow winding stream beds.

This area connects with the St. Lawrence Slope region, a narrow band of resistant Early Carboniferous rocks stretching from Margaree Harbour to Cape North. Pleasant River flows along a fault to the Northumberland Strait.

Softwoods, spruce, hemlock, pine, and fir predominate, but maple and birch also grow in the area. Stands of white spruce occur on old fields, while tolerant hardwoods, sugar maple, yellow birch and beech, grow on better drained slopes and rich intervale soils.

Numerous barachois ponds (triangular beaches enclosing a small lagoon) are found here. Freshwater habitats support diverse fauna. Several bird species, including bald eagles and Black Guillemots, are common here.

Until 1927, Pleasant Bay was reachable only by water or by a narrow footpath over the mountains. The inhabitants, mostly of Scottish or English descent, do some farming but fishing is their livelihood. The area around Pleasant Bay contains the oldest sugar maple stand (300 years old) in Atlantic Canada.

After leaving Pleasant Bay, the trail swings eastward up the slopes of North Mountain, rising to an elevation of 445 m (1,460 ft) before beginning its descent into the beautiful valley of the North Aspy River. There are several look-offs along the road.

Activities: Cape Breton Highlands National Park   3.7.1
Hike Fishing Cove

Cape Breton Highlands National Park features twenty-eight trails of tantalizing scenery. These trails were originally used by the Micmac and early European settlers as the only land links between settlements. No automobiles ventured into the Highlands until 1926, and, even today, motorized vehicles only reach the edges of the park.

One of the first trails on your agenda is the one to Fishing Cove, which lies 350 m (1148 ft) below the look-off of MacKenzie Mountain. Be prepared for a challenging 9 km (5.6 mi.) hike along the river valley. Once, Fishing Cove was a thriving fishing and farming community, complete with a lobster cannery, but by 1915, descendants of the pioneer Scottish settlers had moved to surrounding communities. The grassy clearing at the end of the trail is all that remains of their presence. Highland hills and thick spruce forests have always isolated

Cape Breton's Scottish heritage is reflected in the sound of the bagpipes.

Cape Breton
Island Coast

Cape Breton communities. Although the modern highway intrudes, you can still sense the isolation of the early settlers.

To get to Fishing Cove, follow the familiar hiker sign about 12 km (7.5 mi.) past the Corney Brook hike, a 6 km (3.7 mi.) hike along a fiercely flowing brook that leads to a waterfall. Wilderness camping is available at Fishing Cove but backpackers require permits (obtain one at Cheticamp Visitor Centres). If you are camping, remember your wool socks, rain gear, and warm sweater, as the Nova Scotian evenings can become chilly. Don't forget insect repellant.

If you don't plan to camp at Fishing Cove, two campgrounds are located only a few kilometres ahead at Pleasant Bay and MacIntosh Brook where another hike awaits you.

3.7.2   Map: Fishing Cove Trail

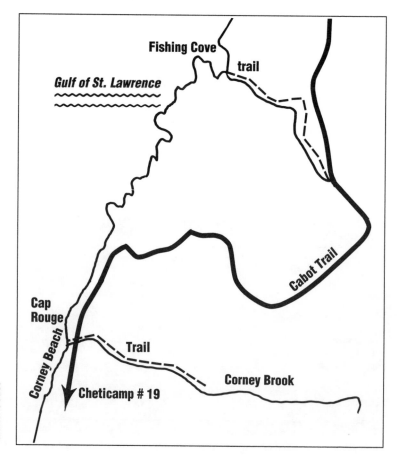

Area: Lowland Cove, Cape North, and Neil's Harbour — Steep Slopes   3.8

The Steep Slopes region is characterized by the margins of the Cape Breton Highlands which are marked by steep slopes and deep valleys. Where the slopes intersect the coastline, cliffs rise up from the sea. There is a very sparse supply of sediments and where they occur beaches are extremely narrow.

Eastern hemlock and white pine dominate on higher slopes, giving way to early successional white birch, white spruce and balsam fir where slopes are unstable or valley bottoms have been disturbed. Along the western coast the steep slopes are exposed to the influence of the Gulf of St. Lawrence. Trees are often stunted by salt spray and winds. Insects and disease have reduced beech stands in this area quite dramatically.

Arctic-alpine plants are found, especially on wet, north-facing canyon rock walls and in other shady, moist habitats. These include Rusty, Smooth and Alpine Woodsia, Common Bladderfern, Willowherb, Western Rattlesnake-Plantain, Northern Bedstraw and Sweet Cicely.

Hardwood forest, conifers, talus slopes, cliffs, and moist valley bottoms provide productive habitat for small animals including Gaspé Shrew, Rock Vole and Weasel. The steep slopes inhibit the movement of larger mammals, although deer make use of the hardwood browse in more accessible areas. Warblers, nuthatches, and woodpeckers thrive on the diversity of vegetation in mature hardwood stands.

Neil's Harbour is a fishing village with a wharf, a beach, and small pond. A popular place for photographers and artists, it is also a good spot to buy fresh fish and lobster from fishermen at their wharves.

Area: Meat Cove to Cape North — St. Lawrence Slope   3.9

Meat Cove at the northernmost coastal section is a continuation of the St. Lawrence Slope. Cape North, the most northerly point on the Cabot Trail, has a museum and was the site of the first Cape Breton-to-Newfoundland undersea telegraph cable, laid in 1856 and used until 1867. The highest cliffs in Nova Scotia are found along this wild, rugged, isolated coastline. Offering the most spectacular back country hiking in the province, it is one of the few remaining coastal wilderness areas in Nova Scotia.

At Aspy Bay, the site of an abandoned gypsum quarry is visible. Swimming and clam digging can be enjoyed on the sandy beaches and there are two lighthouses operating at both ends of the sand bar. Whale-watching cruises operate out of Bay St. Lawrence.

Cabot's Landing Provincial Park provides access to a barrier beach and a

Cape Breton Island Coast

view of Aspy Bay, North Harbour, and the North Aspy River. The steep slopes of the North Aspy Valley are covered by a climax beech forest.

3.9.1 Activities: Meat Cove
Back Country Hiking

Meat Cove is at the end of the road where the St. Lawrence Seaway meets the Atlantic Ocean near the high cliffs at Cape St. Lawrence, second only to Cape North as the most northerly tip of Cape Breton. Here and in nearby Bay St. Lawrence, you'll find some of the most remote back country hiking in Cape Breton. Eleven hiking trails will take you to places of spectacular scenery and abundant wildlife. The McLellan family, who will be your hosts, have lived and fished in Meat Cove for six generations, and can give you information on hiking trails, summer activities, and area history. They also provide fresh seafood; arrange deep sea fishing, whale- and bird-watching tours; and see that your stay in Meat Cove becomes a lasting memory.

The hikes vary from 1 km (.6 mi.) to 30 km (18.6 mi.) and will take you along the coastline, where resistant rocks keep the inclines sharp, and through one of Nova Scotia's last wild areas where bald eagles, moose and bear still live.

To get to Meat Cove, exit left at Cape North and continue approximately 2 km (1.2 mi.) past Bay Road Valley where you'll turn left at the fork in the road past Capstick to Meat Cove. Non-hikers can amuse themselves whale-watching at Bay St. Lawrence and clam digging at Cabot Beach.

Back country hiking well above sea level.

Cape Breton
Island Coast

Map: Hiking Trails of Northern Cape Breton   3.9.2

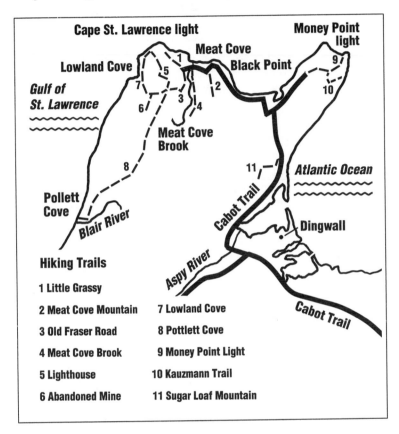

Cape St. Lawrence light

Money Point light

Meat Cove

Lowland Cove

Black Point

Gulf of St. Lawrence

Meat Cove Brook

Atlantic Ocean

Pollett Cove

Blair River

Aspy River

Cabot Trail

Dingwall

Cabot Trail

Hiking Trails

1 Little Grassy

2 Meat Cove Mountain   7 Lowland Cove

3 Old Fraser Road   8 Pottlett Cove

4 Meat Cove Brook   9 Money Point Light

5 Lighthouse   10 Kauzmann Trail

6 Abandoned Mine   11 Sugar Loaf Mountain

Area: Aspy River, Ingonish River, and St. Ann's Bay — Victoria Coastal Plain   3.10

The Ingonish area is a recreational paradise. Golf, hiking, swimming, snorkelling, windsurfing, and yachting are all featured in season, while gourmands will appreciate the fine French cuisine at the ever-popular Keltic Lodge.

The Ingonish River and St. Ann's Bay are part of the Victoria Coastal Plain. Just northside of Ingonish, rocks lie directly on top of a substructure of underlying rock, forming a narrow lowland. St. Ann's Bay, further south, is a coastal margin stretching from Cape Smokey to Indian Brook. Kelly's Mountain, to the east, is a parallel upland block and the first challenge for cyclists travelling counterclockwise around the Cabot Trail.

On the flood plains, willow, aspen, sugar maple and yellow birch are found,

Cape Breton Island Coast

65

while on better drained gravels, white birch and beech occur. On the granite slopes, white spruce is common with scattered stands of yellow birch and sugar maple.

Eagles occasionally breed in this area. A moderate-sized heron colony exists in Aspy Bay, which is also visited by a wide variety of waterfowl from spring through fall, though not in large numbers.

Ingonish Beach offers excellent swimming with two supervised swimming areas (one on the ocean, the other at a nearby freshwater lake).

Middle Head is the location of Keltic Lodge, a fine resort hotel operated by the provincial government. The Lodge features a heated saltwater pool, trails, and spectacular views of the Ingonish coastline and surrounding Highlands. The Middle Head Hiking Trail starts at the Keltic Lodge parking lot and winds through spruce forests and meadows to the edge of the peninsula. From here a noisy tern colony can be seen (and heard) atop a high pinnacle.

Other attractions in the Ingonish area include the hiking trail to Mount Franey, the beach at Ingonish Centre, and the Clyburn Brook picnic area and hiking trail.

After the descent from Cape Smokey, the trail continues through small fishing villages such as Wreck Cove, Skir Dhu, and North Shore. The promontory on the left is Cape Dauphin. A short, steep walking trail to the cliff edge affords excellent views of the Bird Islands.

Further along, a road leads off left to Englishtown and the car ferry to join the Cabot Trail at Barachois River Bridge. On either side of Kelly's Mountain, look-offs provide breathtaking views of St. Ann's Bay and the fiord-like Great Bras d'Or. Before crossing Seal Island Bridge, the road left leads to New Campbellton and a hiking trail to the Fairy Hole, a sea cave where, it is said, Glooscap once lived.

The Cabot Trail continues to St. Ann's, known for its high bluffs, sandy shores, and exquisite sea views. Two good trout streams, the North and Barachois Rivers, flow into St. Ann's Harbour and Bay.

At Plaster Provincial Park, with its numerous ponds in sinkholes, a trail leads down from the high bank to the edge of St. Ann's Bay.

South Gut St. Ann's was first settled by Scottish Highlanders, who, in the 1820s, set sail from Pictou intent on finding a new home in the United States. Seeking shelter from a storm shortly after sailing, they stopped in St. Ann's Harbour and decided to stay. The Nova Scotia Gaelic College of Arts and Culture is in St. Ann's and stands on 400 acres of the original 1,000 acres granted to the first settlers. The only Gaelic College in Canada, St. Ann's gives courses in the Gaelic language, Highland dancing, bagpipe playing, clan lore, Gaelic singing, and in handweaving of tartans. The Gaelic Mod, a seven-day festival of Celtic culture, takes place at St. Ann's the first full week of August.

Activities: Cape Breton Highlands National Park   3.10.1
Hike Jigging Cove Lake and Mary Ann Falls

Near Neil's Harbour, on the east side of the Cape Breton Highlands National Park, there are enough hiking opportunities for two-three days of serious walking.

Camping south of Neil's Harbour at Black Brook Cove, you can set out to hike to Neil's Harbour 4.5 km (2.8 mi.) along the coast via South Point, Victoria Beach, and Jigging Cove. At Victoria Beach, turn right for a hike inland to Jigging Cove Lake 2 km (1.2 mi.), then around the lake and backtrack to Victoria Beach 2 km (1.2 mi.) continuing north to the highway at Neil's Harbour 2.5 km (1.6 mi.). Return to your campsite at Black Brook 6 km (3.7 mi.). On your second day you can either take the short hike near the campsite 1 km (.6 mi.), or hike to Mary Ann Falls, 4.5 km (2.8 mi.) away. Begin by driving (or cycling) north from Black Brook Cove about 3 km (1.9 mi.) and watch for the hiking sign to Mary Ann Falls on your left. After a refreshing rest at the falls, either hike back the same route or, if you've arranged for a ride at the falls, return along a secondary road south which joins the Cabot Trail inland from Broad Cove. You can arrange for your camping gear to be transported to Broad Cove from Black Brook Cove where you can spend another two days hiking to Warren Lake and up Broad Cove Mountain before heading on to Ingonish Beach for a recuperative day or so of beach life, golf, and tennis.

Hikers savour the view at Middle Head, Cape Breton.

Cape Breton
Island Coast

3.10.2 Map: Neil's Harbour Hikes

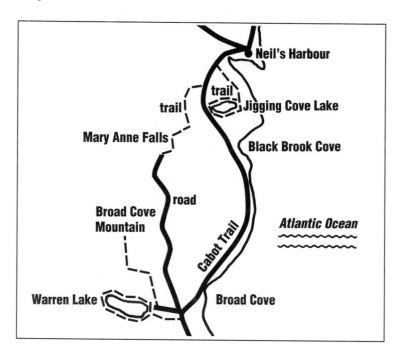

3.10.3 Activities: Ingonish Beach
Explore the Ingonish Area on Foot

Ingonish Beach offers facilities from the rustic to the luxurious, from campfire cookouts and tent living to haute cuisine and four-star suites. It boasts both a freshwater lake and a sandy beach, a superb 18-hole golf course and tennis courts. The park's interpretive centre offers information sessions and guided tours of the natural history present. Park naturalists are always eager to talk about the area's wildlife.

The main hike here is along the Middle Head Peninsula, a place whose geological history goes back millions of years. North and South Bay Ingonish were once covered by sedimentary rock such as shale, gypsum, and sandstone. Erosion eventually carried these soft materials away, leaving only a resistant granite peninsula called Middle Head, a long serpentine land mass stretching out into Bay Ingonish. The 2 km (1.2 mi.) hike takes approximately 45 to 60 minutes. Some of the most arresting features include the rock "gates" near the trail head, a legacy of the previous generations of local inhabitants. Large boulders along the trail are pink granite. A meadow was once the site of a small fishing village. There are spectacular views of Cape Smoky from several points, and birders will want to walk out to Tern Rock (after the breeding season) occupied by hundreds of Common and Arctic Terns. During breeding season, a barricade just before you reach Tern Rock will remind you that the birds are not to be disturbed.

White-tailed deer, Red Fox and Showshoe Hare live on Middle Head, but the setting is more marine. Inshore fishermen keep busy from spring to fall, beginning with the spring trap fishery, followed by salmon season, and finishing with mackerel in late summer and fall.

Offshore, whales may be spotted during July and August, especially the non-toothed Sei Whale and toothed Pilot Whales, called "blackfish" by local fishermen.

For those who prefer hiking with a golf club in hand, Keltic Lodge boasts one of the province's most sophisticated courses.

Map: Ingonish   3.10.4

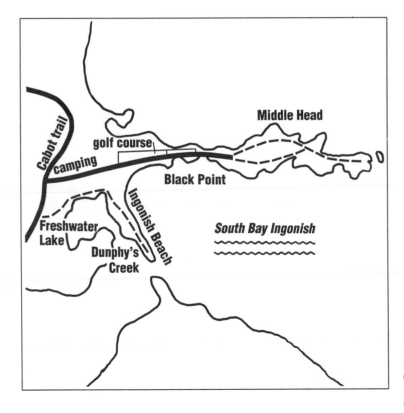

Cape Breton
Island Coast

3.10.5   **Activities: Big Bras d'Or**
Meet the Birds of Bird Islands

Hertford and Ciboux Islands, the Bird Islands, are two small islands near St. Ann's Bay off the eastern coast of Cape Breton Island. Their sharp vertical cliffs provide protection from surface and aerial predators and are important breeding sites for many Atlantic seabirds.

From May to late August, the Atlantic Puffin can be observed brightening the sheer cliffs of the islands with its distinctive markings; from May to early August, the Razor-Billed Auk breeds here and Black Guillemots nest from May to early September. The Black-Legged Kittiwake, the Great and Double Crested Cormorants and the Great Blackback and Herring Gulls are also resident here during these months.

Boat tours to the islands leave daily from Big Bras d'Or, five miles from Exit 16 off Route 105 from Baddeck. The 2 ½ hour tour begins with a 45-minute boat cruise. Fishermen hauling nets, grey seals sunning themselves on rocks or swimming, and Bald Eagles circling their nesting territories are common sights.

Approaching the Islands, the boat slows to a crawl, motoring carefully to avoid disturbing nesting or juvenile birds. The average viewing distance from the Islands is under 18 m (60 ft) so photographers can shoot at close range.

Meeting the birds of Bird Island.

Cape Breton
Island Coast

Map: Baddeck to Big Bras d'Or

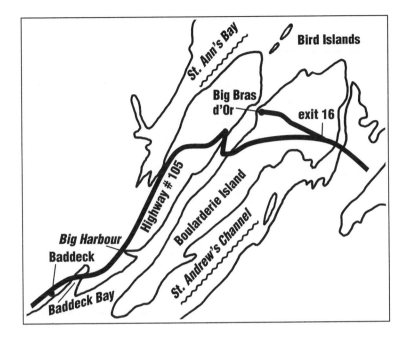

Area: Big Bras d'Or to Mira (Sydney Area) —
Sydney Coal Fields

Industrial Cape Breton is a completely different world from the Highland region. The first region, the Sydney Coal Field, lies within an area of sandstones and siltstones that cover about 1,295 sq. kilometres (500 sq. miles). Coal seams are up to 1,981 m (6,500 ft) thick. The strata have been relatively undisturbed and lie in open folds dipping gently seawards.

The coast offers the best exposures of the coal, although only a few layers can be seen at any one location. One section northwest from Cranberry Point is a 564 m (1,850 ft) vertical section containing 34 coal seams. A 91 cm (3 ft) thick seam is exposed at Point Aconi and abundant plant fossils can be found in the shales on the beach. Some mines extend 8 km (5 mi.) under the Cabot Strait. In total, there are an estimated 1,000 million tonnes of recoverable coal resources off Cape Breton.

This area has a somewhat milder climate than much of the Carboniferous Lowlands, although strong northeast winds retard springtime warming.

There are a few salt marsh areas with eelgrass beds in Lingan Basin, Glace Bay, and Port Morien.

Cape Breton
Island Coast

Some Bald Eagle nesting habitat occurs in this district. The vertical cliffs of the coast provide nesting sites for sea birds and the Bird Islands are important nesting areas for Razorbill, Common Puffin, Leach's Storm Petrel and kittiwakes. Big Glace Bay Lake and Morien Bay provide stopping-over areas for modest numbers of migratory waterfowl, but are of particular importance due to species' diversity. The Piping Plover nests at the Glace Bay Sanctuary. Cormorant breeding colonies occur along the coast.

Industrial Cape Breton includes the area around Spanish Bay and Sydney Harbour, the city of Sydney and the towns of Reserve Mines, Glace Bay, Dominion, New Waterford, North Sydney, and Sydney Mines.

Sydney, situated on a large, protected harbour, is known as "The Steel City" and is Nova Scotia's third largest community. The Marine Atlantic Inc. ferry service to Newfoundland is located at North Sydney at the end of the Trans Canada Highway.

Founded in 1785, the first settlers were Loyalists from New York who were followed 20 years later by immigrants from the Scottish Highlands. Sydney "boomed" at the turn of the century with the building of the Dominion Steel and Coal Company's steel plant at Whitney Pier, the largest self-contained steel plant in North America and still the city's major industry.

New Waterford lies on the edge of the Atlantic near the entrance to Sydney Harbour. The harbour maintains an active fishing fleet which operates from the local wharf. New Waterford was once one of the largest coal-producing areas in the province. In 1925, a bitter strike claimed the life of miner William Davis. A monument on Baker Street tells the story of this tragic event. The Colliery Lands Park is located on the site of the former No. 12 and No. 16 coal mines. A memorial in the park commemorates the 298 miners killed over the years in local collieries. The park features an exposed coal seam, a pipe slope, a coal hopper car display, picnic tables, and a bandshell.

Further along the coast is Glace Bay, a sprawling industrial town known for its extensive coalfields and the sight of the first west-east trans-Atlantic radio message. French troops dug coal from the cliffs at Port Morien near Glace Bay as early as 1720 to supply the garrison at Louisbourg. The Glace Bay Miners' Museum, at the end of Quarry Road at the water's edge, offers underground tours of the Ocean Deeps mine. There is also a reproduction of a miners' village and displays of coal-mining techniques. Glace Bay also has a fishing fleet and a fish processing plant.

Near Glace Bay, Dominion Beach is a good example of a barrier beach that has deteriorated as a result of aggregate extraction and heavy recreational use. The beach is being rehabilitated and will be protected as a provincial park.

Cape Breton
Island Coast

72

Activities: Glace Bay   3.11.1
Visit the Miners' Museum

Nowhere is the precarious interrelationship between the natural world and man more apparent than in the coal mining industry. Coal mining continues to claim the lives of men through accidents and black lung disease, yet no other industry has such a tradition of camaraderie, heroism, songs, and cultural events.

At the famous Miners' Museum in Glace Bay, you can focus on the contribution of the coal miner to both the past and present. The museum features dozens of exhibits documenting the mining industry. Retired miners will be your guides for an engaging tour of the Ocean Deeps Colliery. The Miners' Village on the same site features a company store and a miner's home from the period 1850-1900. The site also serves delicious food at the Miners' Village restaurant.

While in Glace Bay, visit Marconi National Historic Site, featuring a museum which documents Marconi's telegraphic achievements in Cape Breton.

Take in some of the wonderful local musical and dramatic talent at the Savoy Theatre on Union Street. Built in 1927, it is both a community landmark and an active performing arts centre.

Map: Glace Bay   3.11.2

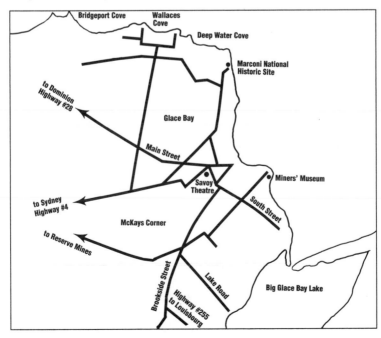

Motor-sailing through St. Peter's Canal.

3.12   Area: Mira to St. Peter's (Louisbourg Area) — Till Plain

South of the industrialized area, Cape Breton turns back time with its reconstructed French fortress and original town structures at Louisbourg, the largest National Park and reconstruction project in Canada.

Louisbourg and surrounding area are situated in the "Till Plain" region, a low-lying, almost flat area with a highly eroded bedrock surface covered with glacial till, sand and gravel. Poor drainage accounts for numerous bogs, swamps, lakes and slow-moving streams. A rocky coastline to the east gives way to barrier beaches in the west. Balsam fir is the dominant tree species with black spruce and larch in wetter areas. Abundant offshore marine life thrives on plankton rich coastal waters. Glacial sands commonly achieve a 100-foot thickness. Drumlins are common.

The Mira River Valley extends from Framboise Cove northwards to Marion Bridge, then sweeps eastward to Mira Bay. The lower reaches of the river have been dammed by glacial gravels to form a long lake. At Mira Bay, the river funnels through a very narrow valley, with steep banks.

Along the coast, white spruce is common, but inland, balsam fir is the dominant species. Hemlock was once common but is now rare, presumably because of selective logging practices of early settlers.

Large bogs are a prominent feature. Bakeapples are found in bogs on

Scatarie Island, on exposed headlands and other coastal bogs and barrens. Heath vegetation, particularly Crowberry, is prevalent.

Sand dune and salt marsh communities with eelgrass beds are found along the coast. Marine flora is generally restricted to cold water specimens.

Staging areas for migratory waterfowl and shorebirds are found along the coast between Fourchu Bay and Framboise Cove. Green Island has the most southerly nesting colony of Black-legged Kittiwakes, the only colony in the Maritime Provinces. Elsewhere, breeding populations of gulls, cormorants, Black Guillemots, and Common Eider can be seen. Pelagic seabird concentrations occur off Louisbourg, and are probably associated with an area of deepwater upswelling.

The Louisbourg Lowland is a cold water coast with little marine fauna. Harbour seals are common; grey seals formerly used Basque Islands for breeding.

At Point Michaud, a proposed ecological site, a beach and sand dune system shows succession from bare sand to white spruce forest.

Scatarie Island is a Provincial Wildlife Management Area with bogs and barrens. Ptarmigan and Arctic Hare have been introduced on the Island.

In the Louisbourg area, bogs, barrens and forests create a patchwork landscape. Residents rely on the fishery for their livelihood, and today there is a fishing fleet and a large fish-processing plant in Louisbourg.

In addition to the famous Fortress of Louisbourg, the town offers crafts inspired by days gone by. The lighthouse on the eastern arm of Louisbourg Harbour is accessible by car and was built near the site of the original lighthouse constructed between 1730 and 1733, making it the second oldest lighthouse in North America.

The fortress stands on the southwestern arm of Louisbourg Harbour covering more than 20 hectares and surrounded by a 1.8 mile-long masonry and earth-packed wall. This was the governmental, commercial and military centre of a colony that included Cape Breton and Prince Edward Islands. The French took more than 20 years to build Louisbourg, and its fortifications were hardly finished when war broke out between England and France in 1745.

Although its defences were weak and its garrisons unprepared, Louisbourg was a constant threat to the New England colonies. It was this threat, combined with commercial, religious and other motives, that encouraged the New Englanders to attack Louisbourg in 1745. William Pepperell, a merchant from Kittery, Maine, commanded an army of volunteers and led his men to victory following a 49-day siege.

Louisbourg was handed back to France by the Treaty of Aix-la-Chapelle (1748), only to be recaptured by the British in 1758. In 1760, just 47 years after the first French settlers had arrived in Louisbourg Harbour. British Prime

Cape Breton
Island Coast

Minister William Pitt ordered the demolition of all the fortifications at Louisbourg.

Parks Canada has restored one-quarter of this 16,549 acre, 18th-century town, including many buildings as well as masonry and earth-packed fortifications.

The Atlantic Statiquarium Marine Museum is a private museum in the town.

Green Island is a nesting site for Black-legged Kittiwakes. Main-a-Dieu has an exposed cobble beach, while at Hilliards Lake, Winging Point Lake, Belfry Lake and Maroche Lake, barachois ponds are enclosed by barrier beaches.

The road continues to Kennington Cove where a cairn marks the landing place of Wolfe in 1758 after his brigade had suffered heavy losses at the hands of the French in Quebec. The road leading to Kennington Cove is believed to have been built by American volunteers during the 1745 siege of the fortress. Big Lorraine, beyond the town of Louisbourg, was a French fishing settlement dating from 1719, and French ruins can still be found here.

Extensive barrier beaches and barachois ponds along this coast, from Red Cape to Cape Gabarus, create one of Nova Scotia's wildest coastal areas. The coast then becomes St. Peter's Bay and continues on to the Isle Madame area.

3.12.1 Activities: Point Michaud
Explore a Beach Ecosystem

The well-known line from an old Scottish ballad, "Oh, ye'll take the high road and I'll take the low road" could well apply to the two distinctively different halves of Cape Breton Island. The highlands to the north and west, the lowlands to the south and east are like fraternal twins—part of the same family but bearing no resemblance to one another.

While the Highlands have their attractions, the lowland coast has also much to offer. In addition to the Louisbourg experience, there are numerous hiking opportunities at the various points or capes along its coast—Main à Dieu, Cape Breton, Cape Gabarus, Fourchu, Point Michaud and Heath Head.

After spending ample time in Louisbourg, travel east along Route 4 (take Route 22 from Louisbourg to exit 8 on Route 125 and turn left onto Route 4 at exit 6). At St. Peters turn left onto Route 247 to Point Michaud Beach, a fantastic long sandy expanse formed by two crescent-shaped sand beaches sweeping landward from a rocky headland. Here you can explore a dune succession from bare sand to white spruce forest. Beach access is provided through Point Michaud Provincial Park where a 2-mile long sandy beach is backed by marram-covered sand dunes and large cranberry bogs. Explore the beach and sandbars or hike out to Point Michaud Point.

Map: Lousibourg to Point Michaud

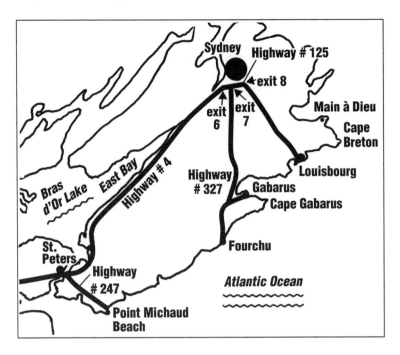

Area: St. Peter's to Port Hastings
(Isle Madame Area) — Sedimentary Lowland

The Sedimentary Lowland area includes the coast around Chedabucto Bay, the largest bay on the Atlantic Coast. Jutting out into the bay is Isle Madame, joined to the mainland by a causeway. This part of the Atlantic Coast is sheltered, and warmer summer water temperatures support several southern marine fauna species.

The shape of the bay owes to the presence of the Chedabucto Fault on the southern side which extends across central Nova Scotia from the Bay of Fundy to the Canso Peninsula. This fault line, the Strait of Canso and Chedabucto Bay itself were probably part of a major river system which rose on the continental shelf and flowed northwards into the Gulf of St. Lawrence during the Triassic and Cretaceous periods. Later, tilting and submergence drowned the valley, creating both the Bay and the Strait. Erosion provides abundant coastal sediment for numerous small gravel beaches. The beaches often enclose small lagoons or salt marshes.

The coastal forest includes white spruce, balsam fir, maple and birch. On

Cape Breton
Island Coast

clay soils, balsam fir and black spruce are dominant, with scattered intolerant hardwoods. Some aspen also occur, especially in disturbed areas. Barrens and bogs are common, particularly on Isle Madame. Old farmland is found mainly on the clay soils, and is mostly regenerating in pure white spruce.

The Bay is not a very productive area for waterfowl or seabirds, because the islands are populated, and sea ice in winter restricts feeding in open water. However, the salt marsh and estuary areas offers habitat for some wading birds (chiefly herons) and shorebirds. Construction of the Canso Causeway in 1955 interfered with species' movement between the Bay and the Gulf of St. Lawrence.

If you are proceeding counterclockwise from Louisbourg, you will arrive at the settlement of L'Ardoise where The Festival Acadien de L'Ardoise is held every July.

St. Peters is situated on a narrow strip of land separating the Atlantic Ocean and Bras d'Or Lake. It was originally used as a portage by the Micmac. Nicholas Denys, a French explorer, established a fishing and fur-trading post here in 1650, and, for 19 years, conducted a variety of commercial enterprises, including the export of lumber to France.

Across the isthmus separating Bras d'Or Lake from the ocean, Denys cut a road so boats could be hauled from the sea to the lake, a project that was repeated 200 years later when the St. Peter's Canal was built. The narrow, one-lock canal took 63 years to build. It shortens the journey for vessels entering the lake from the southwest. The tidal activity at both ends of the canal required that both entrances have double-lock gates. The Nicholas Denys Museum, located on the west bank of the canal, is open in the summer and tells the story of this enterprising pioneer.

Battery Provincial Park is located across the canal from St. Peter's.

River Bourgeois is an Acadian settlement whose inhabitants are descendants of the first Acadians of Cape Breton. The River Bourgeois Historical Society has established a museum with local artifacts.

Louisdale, a large Acadian village, is at the entrance to Isle Madame, a rectangular island you can drive around in less than an hour. It is wooded, but the shoreline offers picnic spots and beaches for swimming.

Lennox Passage Provincial Park has a saltwater beach, an operating lighthouse on a sand spit, and a trail on the top of the bank along the shore.

Martinique was settled by a group of Acadians who were deported during the Expulsion of 1755. Attempts to settle in Martinique in the French West Indies were unsuccessful and many returned to Nova Scotia.

The road continues through D'Ecousse and Pondville to Arichat.

Pondville Beach Provincial Park has a sandy beach backed by gentle

Cape Breton
Island Coast

78

dunes. Behind the dunes lies a large lagoon and salt marsh, habitat for many species of shore birds.

Arichat is one of the oldest settlements in Nova Scotia. It had strong business ties with Jersey and the Channel Islands during the mid-1700s. LeNoir Forge Museum is open in the summer.

Nearby Petit-de-Grat has a wharf and fish plant in the town, which is the oldest settlement on Isle Madame, founded before 1720 by Acadians from Louisbourg. During the French period at Louisbourg, much illicit trade took place when New England vessels brought tar, pitch and planks, which they traded for West Indian rum and molasses. Le Festival Acadien de Petit-de-Grat is held each August.

The coast continues along the shores of Chedabucto Bay until it enters the Strait of Canso, one of the deepest harbours in the world. Port Hawkesbury, formerly called Ship Harbour, is located on the Strait and is an industrial centre. The Nova Scotia Nautical Institute offering instruction in navigation and seamanship, is located here. The Festival of the Strait is a major annual event held during the first week of July.

Port Hastings, at the Canso Causeway, ends the coastal journey around the island.

Activities: Isle Madame   3.13.1
Tour the Island by Foot, Bicycle, or Car

Isle Madame (Route 320 at Grand Anse, west of Louisdale on Route 104) makes for a lovely one or two day hike or bicycle ride. Just over 40 km (27 mi.) around, you can plan on hiking two moderately-paced days, staying at Arichat on the southside where a campground and an Acadian-style inn await you. If you arrive on horseback, you can even have your horse reshod at LeNoire Forge Museum, a restored 18th century blacksmith shop!

Begin your tour at Martinique across the causeway from the main island of Cape Breton where you can pick up information at the centre. You can travel either clockwise or counterclockwise (let the wind decide) making Arichat your first day's destination.

If you opt to travel clockwise, walk or bike to D'Ecousse where you can turn right on Route 320 or continue around the peninsula going as far as Cap La Ronde. This alternate route is approximately 18 km (10.8 mi.) around to Pondville whereas Route 320 is 8 km (14.5 mi.) from D'Ecousse to Pondville. At Pondville, there is a picnic park with sandy beach, dunes, a large lagoon and salt marsh which provides habitat for many different species of shorebirds.

Continue on Route 320 south to the T where a right turn will take you to Arichat. Turning left you can go to Petit-de-Grat (an island off an island off an

Cape Breton
Island Coast

island!), Isle Madame's fishing centre and the site of the oldest settlement (before 1720) on Isle Madame. The route to Petit-de-Grat is approximately 12 km (7.5 mi.) return from the T.

The lighthouse on Green Island off Petit-de-Grat Island is a marker for all ships travelling from points east, and is one of the few remaining manned lighthouses in the province.

Continuing clockwise you'll come to the exit for Port Royal and Janvrin Island, a beautiful island where professional lessons in scuba diving, water skiing and underwater photography are available. Visits to Babin's Hill and Janvrin Harbour will complete your trip to picturesque and historic Isle Madame.

3.13.2 **Map: Isle Madame**

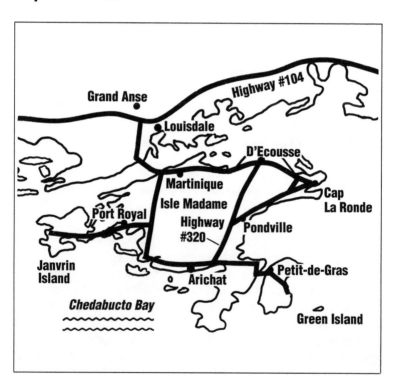

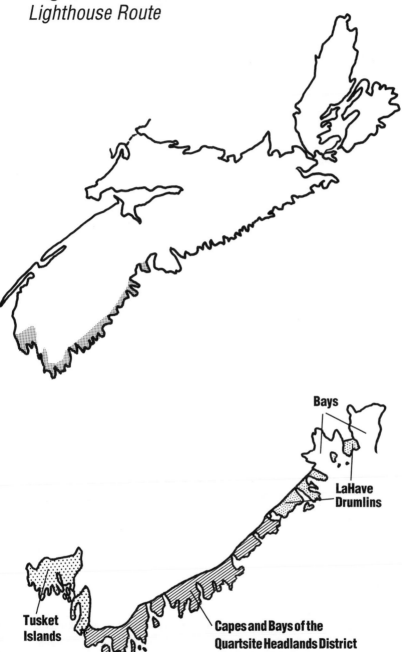

Bays

LaHave
Drumlins

Tusket
Islands

Capes and Bays of the
Quartsite Headlands District

Nova Scotia's South Shore is a mixture of barren granite headlands, erosion carved coves, beaches, and marshes. Every major rock type of Nova Scotia can be found here. Hundreds of islands dot sheltered bays backed by interior forest lands.

The Atlantic Coast's South Shore features the "Lighthouse Trail," and includes both coastal and inland regions. It extends from the town of Yarmouth to Pubnico, including the "Tusket Islands," Cape Sable to Lunenburg, including Tancook Island, and east to Tantallon, including both Mahone and St. Margaret's Bays.

4.1   Area: Yarmouth to Pubnico — Tusket Islands

All along this rugged coast, droning lighthouse horns warn mariners of treacherous shoals and numerous islands, thus the name, "Lighthouse Route." Numerous villages and several towns, largely supported by the fishing industry, span the coastline.

This area of submerged coastline, mild winter temperatures, abundant islands, sheltered inlets, and extensive areas of salt marsh and intertidal sands and muds, provide important wintering habitat for waterfowl and Bald Eagles. Shorebirds begin to arrive in the spring, reaching peak numbers in early to mid-August and declining by September. Osprey breed along this shore, Leach's Storm Petrel breeds on the Tusket Islands, and in summer, the "wee-willa-willet" call of the White-winged Willet can be heard at Chebogue Point.

The highly indented coastline with many elongated islands oriented north to south, was created by submerged ridges formed by the efforts of south-flowing glacial ice on weak bands in the coastal rock formations. Drumlins occur both onshore and as offshore islands. The area has 8,000 acres of salt marsh, a variety of soil conditions and large peat deposits.

Some areas have been cleared for agriculture but normally support good growth of white spruce and balsam fir, with red maple, birch and poplar. Better drained, more sheltered sites may have some pine or oak. Black spruce and larch swamps are common. Due to relatively rapid erosion, the transition from salt marsh to spruce woods is often quite abrupt. A fringe of grey, dead trees usually forms a backdrop behind the salt marshes as the rising sea level drowns their root systems. Examples of the southwestern flora represented here are a bladderwort and Curly Grass Fern.

An area of upwelling offshore, combined with tidal mixing, creates a nutrient-rich marine environment which supports abundant algae, crustaceans, and fish. The warmer waters inshore support a variety of invertebrates, while the Tusket River hosts large runs of Gaspereaux in the spring.

The more fertile inland soils, derived from schists, supply inland waters

Canoeists discover the thrill of off-shore canoeing.

with many nutrients to support diverse freshwater fauna, including molluscs and the Acadian Whitefish.

At Chebogue River and Pinkney's Point, you can see some of the most extensive salt marshes on Nova Scotia's Atlantic coast. At Chebogue Point, there is a fabulous view of the Atlantic and the Tusket Islands. In early summer, the warm colours of wild lupines cast a rosy hue over the landscape.

The Acadian community of Wedgeport, (named for the wedge-shaped point of land on which it stands), was once a major centre for Bluefin Tuna fishing. Today, it is a centre for lobster and inshore fishing. Herring and mackerel feed along the Tusket Tide-Rip, also known as the Soldiers' Rip, a six-knot tide stream about 1.5 km wide (1 mi.), running among the rocky islands.

Tusket gets its name from the Micmac word meaning "the great forked tidal river." The village was settled by Dutch United Empire Loyalists from New Jersey and New York in 1785, although a few Micmac and some Acadian French preceded the Loyalists.

From Central Argyle to the county line, the land is composed of timberland, barrens, and bogs and indented with many lakes and streams, a natural home for fish and big game. The Tusket Islands, numbering approximately 365, (the same as the cluster in Mahone Bay), begin just offshore and are a great area for bird-watching and expansive ocean views.

The residents of Pubnico are mainly descendants of New Englanders who came here after 1761. West, Middle West, and Lower West Pubnico were settled in 1653 by Acadians, making the area the oldest Acadian settlement in the province. All the Pubnicos rely on the sea for their livelihood. There are several wharves, breakwaters, fishing fleets and fish-processing plants in the area.

The islands in the distance off the coast are Seal Island, Mud Island Group, and Johns Island (located closest to the mainland). Seal Island has a lifesaving station, a lighthouse and a wireless station to guide mariners into the Bay of Fundy.

In the Woods Harbour district, where fishing is the major industry, fishermen also collect Irish moss. During the summer months, the moss is unloaded at wharves and transported out of the community for processing.

Provincial parks are located at Glenwood and Upper West Pubnico.

Activities: Pubnico
Bird-watch Around the Tusket Islands

The tip of southwest Nova Scotia, south of Yarmouth, provides some of the best salt marshes on the Atlantic coast. A day can easily be spent biking or driving to the tips of three different points to see the marsh and to bird-watch.

Salt marshes grace the coast with their green calmness, providing "nursery" habitat for primary creatures and food for fish, acting like a biological restaurant. The silt which forms these salt marshes comes from particulate matter carried along the ocean shore. The plant material that grows in this sea-bathed silt is eaten by small snails and other invertebrates. After dying and being ground up by ice and water action into a powdery food, this plant material is taken out to sea by the tide where it is eaten by the first animals in the food chain. Eventually, this essential nutrient reaches fish, bird, and man.

Salt marshes owe their existence to the stiff-leaved marsh grass, unique in its ability to withstand salt water soakings. The tough roots hold the surface against erosion, matting the mud to the bottom.

Because of the warm protectiveness of salt marshes, many species of insect, fish, and animal breed and develop in their midst. Birds of many types, including migratory varieties, waterfowl and shorebirds, as well as other species such as members of the Oriole family, which have been sighted here but rarely elsewhere in the province, feed in this haven of living forms.

Begin your travels in Yarmouth, Nova Scotia's most southerly region. Pack a good lunch, and leave Yarmouth by following Main Street south past the Nova Scotia Information Centre and on to Chebogue Point. At Rockville, turn right and continue south, a total distance of approximately 15 km (9.3 mi.). Park your car or bike by the side of the road and wander into nearby marshy areas for a closer look at *spartina alterniflora* (marsh grass) and the simple joy of bird-watching.

Backtrack to Rockville about 5 km (3 mi.) and turn right, heading east to Arcadia (Route 334) along the Chebogue River. Watch for staddles, sticks in the marsh grass traditionally used for stacking marsh hay. Inquire at local stores for marsh greens or "goose tongues" as they are sometimes called. About 2.5 km (1.6 mi.) past Arcadia, turn right toward Pinkney's Point, a drive through an area which is inundated with lakes, drowned estuaries of rivers and harbours. From atop this point you can see the Tusket Islands. Here also, salt marsh abounds.

Continue 4 km (2.5 mi.) until you reach a fork at Melbourne. Bear right at the fork and go on to Pinkney's Point, about 10 km (6.2 mi.). Have your lunch and a walk around the area before returning to Yarmouth via Kelly's Cove (1.5 km (.9 mi.) past Rockville where you bear right to Yarmouth). Enjoy sightseeing

The Atlantic Coast's South Shore

85

and shopping in downtown Yarmouth. (The fried clams at the local diner aren't to be missed.) A drive to Cape Fourchu, directly south of Yarmouth, for the sunset will end a perfect day in and around salt marsh country.

4.1.2   Map: Cape Forchu to Pinkney's Point

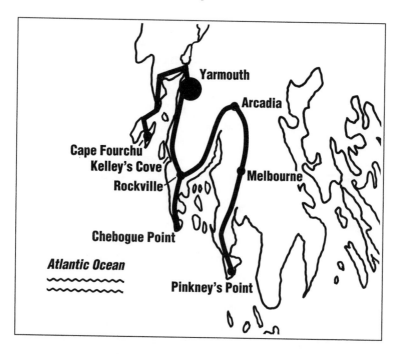

4.2   Area: Cape Sable Island to Lunenburg — Capes and Bays

The capes and bays of this area are dominated by a rock known as greywacke with granite intrusions. Throughout this area they form a hummocky terrain with little relief. The bays are drowned river estuaries.

Sand is abundant, however, since it was carried landward from offshore glacial material when sea levels rose. This coastal area experiences strong winds and powerful waves. Barrier beaches and dune systems are subject to periodic destruction during storms. The sand is either carried seawards into deep water or over the beach into lagoons as overwash. Wide expanses of flat beach areas are subject to erosion from wind, which eventually creates dunes further inland.

Large areas of bog and barren are the result of low relief, fire and the

The Atlantic Coast's
South Shore

86

accumulation of organic materials. Labrador Tea, Lambskill, and blueberries provide the main vegetative cover on the barrens. Elsewhere, the forest is chiefly white spruce and balsam fir with maple, birch, and poplar. Some pine and red oak can be found on better drained sites further inland. In wet, peaty areas black spruce, larch and alders are found.

Coastal habitats include many sand beaches, salt marshes, intertidal muds, and sands at the heads of longer inlets and cobble beaches. Rocky shores are mostly confined to the shoreline between Liverpool and Port Medway. This section of the coast is on the route for migratory waterfowl and shorebirds.

Offshore, nutrient-rich waters provide food for overwintering pelagic seabirds and whales. In the summer, warm water incursions from the Gulf Stream often bring exotic tropical species to the beaches and inlets in this area.

From the Chapel Hill Museum at Shag Harbour at night, you can see the lights of five lighthouses: Cape Sable, Bon Portage Island, Seal Island, Baccaro Point, and Woods Harbour. By day, observe the far-reaching view of the sea with its islands dotting the horizon.

At Archelaus Smith Museum, at Newellton, you can view artifacts of local history relating to lobster fishing and shipbuilding.

Cape Sable Island, the most southerly portion of Nova Scotia, is well-known for bird-watching and the home of the famous Cape Island boat, first built by Ephraim Atkinson at Clark's Harbour in 1907. Today, it sets the standard in a small boat for high stability and efficiency in the North Atlantic. From Clark's Harbour, Cape Sable lighthouse is accessible by boat.

Barrington provides excellent yachting, swimming, and hiking trails. Once a thriving Acadian settlement, it was burned and ransacked by the English in 1758. It has four museums, including Barrington Woollen Mill and the Cape Sable Historical Society Centre housed in its lighthouse.

The Baccaro lighthouse is accessible by car. The Cape Roseway lighthouse on McNutt's Island at the entrance of Shelburne Harbour can only be reached by motorboat.

A gravel road near Roseway leads to Roseway Beach, a large expanse of fine, clean sand, sand bars, and shallow inlets. Many shorebirds populate the beach from June to August.

Shelburne, the Loyalist Town, was once one of the largest communities in North America. Thousands of British subjects fled from the colonies when hostilities began between Britain and America and settled in Shelburne. Those who remained after 1787 built the town into a major fishing and shipbuilding centre.

Today, many "Loyalist" artifacts and paintings are on display in the Ross-Thompson House (1784). The Rudolph–Williams House (1787) has been renovated as the Shelburne County Museum and contains important exhibits depicting Shelburne's shipbuilding and Loyalist heritage.

Near Shelburne is the Tobeatic Wildlife Management Area, covering the headwaters of the Mersey, Jordan, Roseway, Clyde, and Tusket Rivers. The area is a maze of lakes which are a delight to canoeists and camera buffs.

Port Joli and Port l'Hebert are resting places of large numbers of Canada Geese because eelgrass, their main food, is plentiful. Here, three migratory bird sanctuaries and two national wildlife reserves have been established.

Lockeport has a mile of hard, sand beach and East Side Port l'Hebert has a long sheltered white sand beach bordered by pine and spruce groves. Nearby lies an old Micmac campsite where arrowheads and tools have been discovered.

Port l'Hebert Pocket Wilderness has been developed with a 3-km (2 mi.) interpretive trail and picnic area.

Near Port Joli and Port Mouton is the Kejimkujik Seaside Adjunct National Park with its unspoiled coastline, dunes, beaches, salt marshes, tidal estuaries, headlands, birds, and seals. Coastal trails are marked for hikers.

Central Port Mouton, which received its name when, in 1604, a sheep was lost overboard a vessel, is now a fishing village with a fish processing plant and a longliner fleet. The top of the hill offers a great view of the bay. During the American Revolution and later during the War of 1812, privateers anchored in the bay, waiting to ambush American vessels bound for Boston.

Liverpool's privateers and their famous vessels, *Lucy, Rover* and *Liverpool*

Canoeist on the Mersey River.

Packet, roamed the seas upholding the British naval traditions of war. Many stately homes in Liverpool's tree-lined streets date back to the privateering era and "widow's walks" are still a prominent feature on many houses. The local museum is Perkins House, built in 1766, which includes the Thomas Raddall (a well-known Canadian author) Research Room for county genealogical data. Deep-sea fishing and boat trips can be arranged from the town. There are also public boat ramps in Liverpool Harbour.

The Western Head lighthouse is accessible by road along the rugged coastline.

Along the coast to Port Medway, you can take a scenic drive through Beach Meadows where you can view Coffin Island and its lighthouse from a distance. A long beach at Beach Meadows has fine white sand and a picnic area.

At Port Medway, the "Blessing of the Fleet" takes place each August. Wreaths of flowers are thrown out to sea in remembrance of those who have perished and to offer prayers for those who still make their living at sea.

Provincial parks are located at Port Joli, Broad River, Summerville Beach, Summerville Centre, Western Head, Liverpool and at Shepards Island outside Shelburne. At Sand Hills Beach Provincial Park, you will find one of the finest beach and dune systems in the area.

Activities: Sand Hills   4.2.1
Explore a Beach and Dune System

During June and July lupins are in bloom everywhere. Irises appear in swampy depressions and bogs, and beach pea shows its variegated blooms.

Sand Hills is a superb outing for nature lovers, joggers, strollers, artists, and swimmers. It provides a wide, broad expanse of fine white sand to run or walk on, to model into sculptures and castles, and to shelter the eggs of the Piping Plovers, one of Nova Scotia's most endangered species. Next to the white ridges of soft sand, other habitats flourish; the picnic area tops a highly-developed dune system, while inland there are cranberry marshes, a bog system, a tidal estuary, a salt marsh, and a sand spit.

To reach Sand Hills, head east along Route 3 from Yarmouth for a leisurely drive or bike through the Argyles and the Pubnicos. You'll need an early start to reach Sand Hills for a noon picnic, so if you're pressed for time, take Route 103 to Barrington. On Route 3, follow the coast via Shag Harbour to connect with Route 103 about 2.5 km (1.6 mi.) before Barrington where you turn right, go 6.5 km (4 mi.) and turn right for 1.5 km (.9 mi.) to the park. You will be astounded how white, fine, and expansive the sand beach is. This important home of bird and plant life requires care from visitors because there are fragile blooms and eggs hidden on its surface.

The Atlantic Coast's
South Shore

After a full afternoon of beach life (don't forget your sun screen), retire to a campsite or one of the fine inns in the area. Shelburne offers good lodging and dining, as well as museums, a genealogy centre, barrel making, and antiques. It's about 40 km (24.9 mi.) east on Route 103.

4.2.2   Map: Yarmouth to Sand Hills Beach

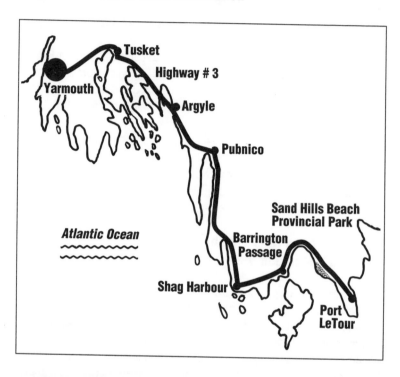

4.2.3   Activities: Roseway
Canoe the Rivers Jordan, Roseway, Sable, and Clyde

The rivers of southwest Nova Scotia, the Mersey, Clyde, Roseway, Jordan, Sable, and Tusket have offered exceptional trout fishing in their time but their numbers have gradually been reduced from the effects of acid rain.

Despite the loss of fishing here, it is still an adventure to explore and enjoy these waters by canoe and there are organized day trips, and longer trips for beginners and experts alike. The season begins "post black fly," between early June and late October. You can learn the fundamentals of canoeing, or, if you know the basics, you can "enrol" for 1, 3, 5 or 7-day trips along the Clyde and the upper waters of the Roseway Rivers. Wilderness canoeing and horseback riding are all components of this adventure. Your guide can also suggest trips on other rivers in the area. Contact Lee Keating (902-637-3719) for further information.

Map: The Rivers of Shelburne County

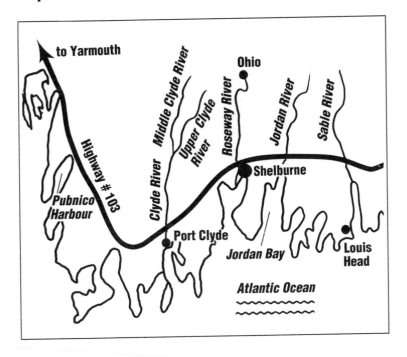

Activities: Liverpool
Deep Sea Fish the Atlantic, and Go Inland to Kejimkujik

This fishing adventure involves boats and, of course, being "out on the water."

After a morning exploring the museums of Liverpool, rent your charter boat from the wharf at Market Street in Liverpool or travel west approximately 18 km (11.2 mi.) to Port Mouton where charters are also available. You'll sail out the harbour, formed when the seaward-drifting glacial ice left behind long ridges and valleys, into the great Atlantic, home to a variety of fish stocks, seabirds, sea mammals, and shipwrecks. Once out of the harbour you can hand-line for cod, haddock, and pollack, or rod and reel for shark. You'll see whales, seals, and seabirds; you'll explore the craggy coastline, and spend quality time on a secluded island beach before heading home as the sun dips toward the horizon. If diving is your pleasure and you are experienced and outfitted, you

The Atlantic Coast's South Shore

can spend the afternoon exploring several of the charted wrecks in the area.

After dinner and a stroll in the town, rest up for tomorrow's trip inland to Kejimkujik National Park, a scenic cross-country drive along Route 8 through wooded country, dotted with lakes. Visit MacGowan Lake Fish Hatchery near Kempt before entering the park for several days of camping, canoeing, and hiking in Nova Scotia's inland national park.

4.2.6   Map: Port Joli to Kejimkujik

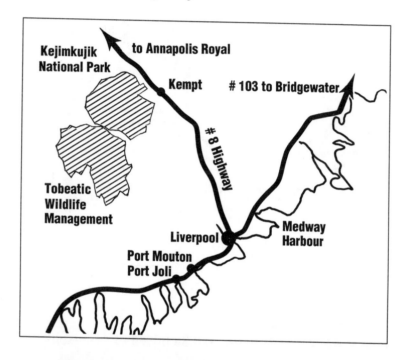

4.3   Area: Lunenburg to Tancook Island (coastal peninsula and islands) — LaHave Drumlins

In the LaHave Drumlin area between Voglers Cove and Aspotogan, the shoreline is a mosaic of rocky, cobble, and sand beaches, interspersed with tidal flats and salt marshes. This patchy shoreline was created by glacial activity, dating back at least 11,000 years. Coastal drumlins (egg-shaped hills) are among the most remarkable physical features in the district. Inland, drumlins have been cleared and farmed; offshore, they form wooded islands with rounded profiles.

There are two main types of drumlin soil. To the west of the LaHave River, drumlins are derived from slate and are characterized by shaley loam soils. To the east, drumlin materials are finer textured, reddish, sandy clay loams. Geologists believe these soils, which make up most islands (except Cape LaHave which is rock), originated in New Brunswick.

White spruce and balsam fir are the dominant species along this coast, but some maple and birch are intermixed in more sheltered locations. Pure stands of white spruce may be found on some drumlins and on old fields. Further inland, spruce, fir, and pine forest occur. Salt marsh and eelgrass beds are common.

The areas around Cape LaHave Island to Rose Bay and the western shore of Mahone Bay at Blue Rocks are locally important as waterfowl and shorebird habitat. Black Duck, Common Goldeneye, Oldsquaw, and Scoter are sometimes present in significant numbers. The Red-necked Grebe overwinters in this area. From early August through September, shorebirds congregate at Crescent Beach and Cherry Hill Beach. Piping Plovers breed at Cherry Hill Beach and Kingsburg Beach. Pearl Island (a provincial Wildlife Management Area) is regionally important because it provides breeding habitat for the Common Puffin, Leach's Storm Petrel, Razorbill, and Black Guillemot. Gulls, cormorants, terns, and the Great Blue Heron breed on other islands along the coast.

Voglers Cove, a small fishing village named after a German settler, has a rugged shoreline. Nearby Cherry Hill has a good beach for collecting shells and driftwood. Broad Cove leads to Beach Road where surf and sand perpetually wear into smaller particles the glacial materials deposited eons ago. The craggy coastline continues to Green Bay, Petite Riviere, and Crescent Beach.

Petite Rivière was first settled in the 1630s by Isaac de Razilly. The drumlin hill on which it sits overlooks the river valley and the LaHave Islands to seaward. At Green Bay, you will find snug, intimate beaches. At Crescent Beach, a sign directing you to the LaHave Islands leads to the Marine Museum on Bell Island.

Nearby is Risser's Beach Provincial Park, containing several habitats, including a mile-and-a half long dune and a salt marsh. These fragile ecosystems were created from glacial sediments which accumulated along the shore. On the primary (or most seaward) dune, pioneering beach plants such as American Beachgrass, Sea Rocket, Sandwort and Orach are abundant. These plants hold and stabilize the loose sand, thus promoting dune development. Further inland, older, more stable dunes support white pine, white spruce, red oak, maple and an undergrowth of Marram Grass, bayberry and moss.

On the sheltered side of the beach, a salt marsh hosts many flora and fauna, including spiders, blue mussels, white clams and small Pink Crabs. Meadowlarks and Myrtle Warblers sing from the bayberry at the edge of the marsh. Overhead, dragonflies hover on a quest for insects. The Petite River,

The Atlantic Coast's South Shore

flowing southwest of the salt marsh, is one of only two rivers in the world inhabited by the Acadian Whitefish.

When the tide is out, the mud flats attract gulls, crows, willets, sanderlings, Semi-Palmated Plovers and White-Rumped Sandpipers. Great Blue Herons perpetually stand guard in shallow water.

A protective sand bar at the mouth of the bay, visible only at low tide, has built up over the years from silts carried downstream by the Petite River. The head-on collision between opposite tidal and river flows caused some materials, mostly sand, to drop to the bottom. The sand bar is changing continually and therefore is relatively free of vegetation. Clams thrive in this sandy habitat and at low tide, especially during June and July, clam digging can be highly rewarding. As the summer wears on, however, large clams become scarce and regulations prohibit harvesting clams under 5 cm (2 in) in diameter.

Risser's Beach is a great place for camping, swimming, beachcombing and geological exploration. Varying rates of erosion, exposing different rocks and minerals, create a ridge and valley effect, offering a variety of fossil specimens.

There is a ferry linking the shores of the LaHave River. A drive along the banks of the wide LaHave River affords the traveller an interesting variety of land and seascapes. Riverport is a village at the mouth of the LaHave River with a large wharf and fish plant. Near here is The Ovens Natural Park, a series of large caverns created by wave action against the rocky cliffs. At West LaHave is the LaHave Yacht Club, where visiting mariners are welcome.

If you arrive in Bridgewater towards the end of July, the South Shore Exhibition and International Ox Pull will be under way. This annual event features agricultural, forestry, craft, and musical displays and demonstrations. The DesBrisay Museum National Exhibition Centre, situated in 10 ha (25 acres) of parkland is also a worthwhile stop if you want to learn more about Lunenburg County's natural and cultural history.

The grand old town of Lunenburg is built on a peninsula and features a front and a back harbour. It was originally a settlement of German and French turnip farmers and artisans who King George II enticed out of Prussian Hanover and Montbeliard, France, in 1753. The transformation of these farmers to offshore fishermen is surely one of the most remarkable metamorphoses of history. The transition has been so complete that nearly everyone assumes the town has a seafaring heritage. The legacy of Lunenburg's founding fathers is the distinctive Lunenburg dialect, a cross between a Southern drawl and a German accent.

The tang of smoked herring and salt cod, the sting of sauerkraut and the spiciness of Lunenburg sausage are strong reminders that this is a place with a distinctive cultural heritage. A town that built the original *Bluenose* schooner

Big Tancook Island, only a ferry ride from Chester, is the largest of Mahone Bay's 365 islands.

The Airlie, the last of the traditional fishing schooners built on Big Tancook.

in 1921, its replica in 1963, and the *H.M.S.Bounty* for the Marlon Brando version of *Mutiny on the Bounty* (not to mention hundreds of other remarkable vessels), also boasts the sturdy dory said to be "as perfectly shaped as a gull."

Today, fishing is still the dominant industry of Lunenburg but fish stocks have gradually declined with the introduction of highly efficient industrial fishing technology (side and stern trawlers and draggers).

No trip to Lunenburg is complete without a visit to the Fisheries Museum of the Atlantic, located on the waterfront. The museum features *Theresa E. Connor,* the last of the salt-bank schooners, and *Cape Sable,* a steel-hulled trawler.

The presence of a vital artistic community is evident from the fine crafts and music produced in the region. The annual Lunenburg Craft Fair and the Lunenburg Folk Harbour (Music) Festival are events not to be missed during the summer months.

Nearby Blue Rocks, remarkable for its blue-grey slate and sandstone ledges, is a picturesque fishing village and a favourite spot for artists and photographers.

At the mouth of Mahone Bay, Big and Little Tancook and East Ironbound form a trio of rocky, rounded island sentinels. Big Tancook, 8.1 km (5 mi.) out from Chester, is the largest of Mahone Bay's 365 islands. The island is famous for its schooner-building and oversize cabbages (said to weigh up to 25 lbs.). Today, only a few of the sturdy little schooners are afloat (replaced by Cape Islanders), but island sauerkraut is still a delicacy for many connoisseurs. Ironbound, four miles beyond Tancook, is the setting for a classic maritime novel, *Rockbound,* by Frank Parker Day.

Although the islands are now most frequently associated with fishing, the original settlers, mostly of German origin, were farmers. They settled on these islands partly because their livestock could range freely and fences weren't necessary. The land was well-treed so that building materials and firewood were readily available. The settlers soon discovered that, once cleared and fertilized with seaweed and fish, the land produced abundant hay and vegetable crops.

The ferry service between the Tancooks and Chester is a relatively new convenience (islanders first requested a government-run or subsidized ferry service in 1934). Even today, travel between the islands and the mainland can be difficult, particularly during winter months when the seas are choppy and the winds fierce. Residents recall severe winters at the turn of the century when the bay froze over, allowing teams of horses to transport people and goods between the islands and neighbouring Blandford and Chester.

Past the communities of Mahone Bay and Chester, lies the Aspotogan (sometimes called Blandford) Peninsula which divides Mahone Bay from St.

Margaret's Bay. On clear nights, the lights of the Pearl Island, East Ironbound and Cross Island lighthouses are visible. Bayswater Beach, beyond Blandford on St. Margaret's Bay, is a provincial picnic site with a broad, white sand beach. Occasionally, seals can be seen sunning themselves on ledges near the shore.

Activities: The Ovens to Risser's Beach, Lunenburg to Mahone Bay Cycle the Drumlin Shore (2 days)

Thunder Cave is a deep recess on the coast, carved from wave action against shale cliff. Water pours into the narrowing tunnel creating a thunderous pounding so strong the whole cave and surrounding area reverberates. Thunder Cave is only one feature, albeit the most astounding, of the Ovens, a naturally occurring series of tunnels and caves which has been a privately-owned campground for a number of years. The Ovens provides an excellent central location for two bicycle day trips which unwind along shores marked by rolling drumlin hills and fabulous ocean views. These are bicycle rides you shouldn't miss.

You arrive at The Ovens park by travelling east along Route 103 and taking exit 12. Follow Route 3 to Upper LaHave, then take Route 332 to Rose Bay and continue 2 km (1.2 mi.) to a T in the road where you'll turn right toward Feltzen South. Signs will announce The Ovens and The Ovens Natural Park, another 5 km (3.1 mi.) along the road. Pick your campsite, tour the caves, pan for gold at Cunard's Beach, meditate at the chapel in the woods, and enjoy a refreshing sleep lulled by the steady surf.

Day 1 of biking will take you to Risser's Beach, 46 km (29 mi.) return, with its salt marsh trail and inviting waters. From The Ovens, backtrack west to East LaHave along Route 332 and take a short ferry ride to LaHave and a moderate ride along the coastal Route 331 where relaxation awaits you. There's a great bakery at LaHave to stock up on fuel food. Return along the same course and head to bed early for tomorrow's more challenging day.

Day 2 will take you east along Route 332 to Lunenburg where a fisheries heritage museum, harbour charters, a panoramic 18-hole golf course on the area's most prominent drumlin hill, hand crafted gifts in well-stocked stores, and restaurants are among the things to see or do. You may wish to end your bicycling here, play some golf, wander the streets which sport some of Nova Scotia's most unique architecture, and splurge on a boat cruise and/or seafood supper before an evening over at one of the inns, or a cycle back to your campsite.

Or, you may wish to continue on to Mahone Bay (along Route 3 north), another fascinating town which houses a wooden boat festival in August, a

The Atlantic Coast's
South Shore

museum, the famous Zwicker's Inn dining experience, and lots of tales of pirates and privateers.

Here, again, you can sleep over or return to the Ovens. Whichever route you choose, Lunenburg alone or the double leg—Lunenburg and Mahone Bay—you'll return with a shipload of images and memories.

4.3.2   Map: Risser's Beach to Mahone Bay

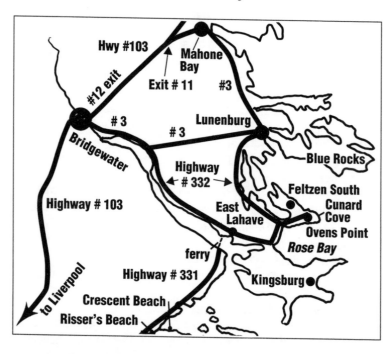

4.3.3   Activities: Lunenburg
Golf and Stroll in the Town of Lunenburg

A full day in Lunenburg involves strolling the drumlin hills of the town, including a walk and some golf atop Lunenburg's largest drumlin, the site of one of the most picturesque golf courses in Nova Scotia. Play a round of golf on the high-rising hill overlooking the harbour before a seafood snack along the waterfront or a picnic of local sauerkraut, Lunenburg pudding or sausage, and home-made bread.

After lunch, immerse yourself in Lunenburg's history with a visit to the Fisheries Museum of the Atlantic. Then head out of town to nearby Blue Rocks, a small fishing village on a stretch of rock and beach. A rewarding activity is searching the shore for fragments of coloured glass, worn smooth and milky by the sea. Local artisans have turned these fragments into jewellery and other crafts and their designs are a fitting memento of the sea's handiwork.

To get to Blue Rocks from Lunenburg, find Lincoln Street and continue all the way down to Blockhouse Hill Road where you turn right, then right again on Sawpit Road, then immediately left onto the road to Blue Rocks, approximately 6 km (3.7 mi.) away. Enjoy the rest of the daylight hours on the beach, sunning, beachcombing, and generally soaking up the ambience before heading back to Lunenburg for dinner at one of the many seafood restaurants in the downtown. A stay over at nearby Ovens Natural Park or Kingsburg, if you're camping, or at one of the fine inns in and around town will complete a truly exceptional "land lubbing" day.

If you plan on a longer stay in Lunenburg, consider a sailing charter to experience big boat sailing. Charters are available for individuals and groups. Inquire at the Fisheries Museum of the Atlantic.

Map: Lunenburg

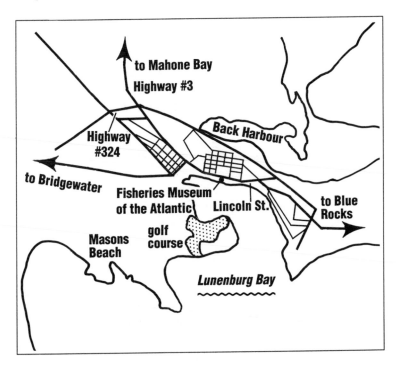

4.4   Area: Lunenburg to Tantallon (along the shores of Mahone Bay and St. Margaret's Bay) — Bays

Mahone Bay and St. Margaret's Bay are two ancient landscape features formed during a period of rapid erosion before the Carboniferous era. During the Middle Carboniferous, the sea extended further inland and deposited limestone and evaporites as it ebbed and flowed. Most of these strata have eroded away and today only a slim rocky fringe remains around the margins of the bays. Granite is the dominant rock-type here, but the series of peninsulas on the west side of Mahone Bay are primarily slate. Blue Rocks is a notable example.

The slates tend to be covered by fairly deep surficial deposits in the form of glacial tills and drumlins. Many drumlins continue into the sea, particularly in Mahone Bay where they form islands known locally as "whalebacks." Graves Island Provincial Park, for example, is located on a drumlin.

Salt marshes, generally low energy environments, are common at the head of Mahone and St. Margaret's Bays. Small, pocket sand beaches occur near exposed coastal headlands.

The vegetation around Mahone and St. Margaret's Bays has been affected by lumbering, but the terrain is essentially a modified coastal forest; mainly softwoods, with red spruce, white spruce and balsam fir.

Coastal waters, particularly in the St. Margaret's Bay area, have been the subject of many oceanographic and biological studies. The deep basin of St. Margaret's Bay, at 76 m (250 ft), is contained by a relatively narrow entrance with a sill at a depth of 36.6 m (120 ft). During the spring, phytoplankton bloom (usually in late April). Nutrient levels in the water's surface layers are replaced during the summer and fall by incursions of nutrient-rich water from the continental shelf, which also brings warm-water animals from the Gulf Stream (e.g., flying fish, seahorse, blue crab). Mackerel and tuna are frequently abundant in the relatively warm waters of Mahone and St. Margaret's Bays.

The western shore of Mahone Bay, including its fringe islands, is locally important as a habitat for waterfowl and shorebirds. From spring through to early winter, Black Duck, Common Goldeneye, Oldsquaw, Scoter and Red-necked Grebe may be sighted. Ospreys are a common nesting bird on several islands.

The shore route brings you to the town of Mahone Bay, a seaside community which offers sailboat and motorboat tours from Mader's Wharf or the Government Wharf around the Bay's numerous islands. The name Mahone is derived from the old French word *mahonne,* meaning a low-lying craft used by pirates. During the War of 1812, the American privateer *Young Teazer* was blown up in Mahone Bay by an English deserter from a British man-of-war. Legend claims that on the anniversary of this event, an apparition known as "the fireship" can be seen drifting in the bay.

Nearby is Indian Point, once a headquarters for the Micmac. An ancient burial ground is located here, and many relics have been found.

Western Shore offers accommodations with a recreation resort and marina. Local residents pursue shore fishing, barrel manufacturing and boat building. Nearby is Oak Island, once covered by heavy oak trees and hence the name. Attempts to locate Captain Kidd's buried treasure here dates back to 1796. Gold River, said to have been the location of gold discoveries by early French settlers, is noted for good salmon fishing during the month of June.

Chester Basin is located on an inlet of Mahone Bay. Principal occupations in the vicinity are lumbering, fishing, farming, boat building, sport fishing, and hunting. A yacht marina is located nearby. Marriotts Cove also boasts a marina with boat haul-out and repair services, as well as dining facilities.

The town of Chester, settled in 1760 by families from New England, is situated on a peninsula at the head of Mahone Bay. Highlights of the summer season are Chester Race Week and Old Home Week, both held in August. Sailing instruction is provided by the Chester Yacht Club, and there is a public boat launch at the Government Wharf.

Crossing the inner reaches of the Blandford Peninsula, you arrive at

Canoeing among the numerous islands of Nova Scotia's south shore.

The Atlantic Coast's
South Shore

Hubbards, once a fishing community but now a mixed economy. Some residents still make their living from the sea while others commute to distant work places, maintaining their homes by the shore. Nearby Queensland offers warm water and three stretches of sandy beaches, including Cleveland Beach, Queensland Beach, and Black Point Beach. At Black Point, the beach has a ramp access for disabled persons. Near the Anglican Church in Queensland, a cairn commemorates the early settlers of St. Margaret's Bay who arrived in the 1780s. Boutilier's Point has a government wharf and a public boat ramp. Many Halifax residents have cottages around the shores of St. Margaret's Bay, long famous as a sailing, boating, and fishing centre.

Head of St. Margaret's Bay is noted for the beauty of its shore scenery. Nearby is the start of the Bowater Mersey Hiking Trail, a place for summer hikers and winter cross-country skiers.

4.4.1   Activities: Mahone Bay
Boat Tour of Mahone Bay

In Mahone Bay, an island exists for every day of the year and some who have fished and boated among them know each one by name. Names denote a local family—Zwicker, Kaulback, Gifford, Rafuse, or a description of what might be found there—Gooseberry, Squid, Birch, Big Fish, Sheep, Spectacle, or what they look like—Round, Clay, Round Nubble. Many have a history that includes ghost stories and local incidents through the centuries.

Before the Europeans came here, the Micmac used the islands for campsites and religious feasts and gatherings.

For a day in the Mahone Bay area, stay at one of the dozen bed and breakfast's available and stroll the "Tri-Church Trail" at the head of the harbour where three churches stand side by side like maiden aunts. Shop for fine arts and crafts and attend the Wooden Boat Festival in August, which will submerge you in the history and craft of boat building, so long a part of this town's livelihood.

In the afternoon, head to those islands on a 42-foot Cape Island fishing boat available for charter (information available at the local tourist centre). Take snacks and beverages on board and remember to bring a warm sweater or jacket, no matter how hot it is on land. Fish and enjoy the freedom of knowing it doesn't matter if you catch any. Stroll the islands and look for birds.

At the end of the day return to land refreshed and relaxed, to enjoy a good meal at one of the local restaurants.

Map: Mahone Bay Coast

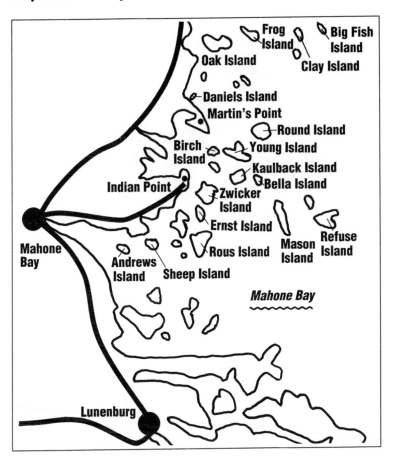

Activities: Chester Basin and Tancook Island
Stroll a Peninsula, Catch a Boat to an Island

Your day begins in Chester Basin, west of Chester, with a morning walk on the Bargel's Point Road. From Mahone Bay, enter Chester Basin and continue to the intersection for Routes 12 and 103. Turn right toward the coast and park your car along the road. The road continues for 2.5 km (1.5 mi.) along a winding sea-lined route among the homes of local and summer residents. Either go to the end of the road and back or continue right at the 2 km (1.5 mi.) point to walk in a loop back to Route 3 where you'll turn right to get back to your car, approximately 3 km (1.9 mi.). After this, head east on Route 3 to Chester and

The Atlantic Coast's South Shore

From windsurfing to blue water racing, St. Margaret's Bay has it all.

take the 45-minute ferry ride to Tancook Island. The ferry sails four times a day (more often on weekends). Be sure *not* to take the last ferry of the day to Tancook if you want to return on the same day as the ferry docks overnight in Tancook. The ferry does not transport cars so you'll be in for some more nice walks on the island. Facilities include a bed and breakfast, canteen, grocery and gift shop, but visitors are encouraged to bring a lunch in case the canteen is closed.

Return to Chester and take in a live theatre performance at the Chester Playhouse from mid-July to late August. If you're in Chester in mid-August, experience Chester Race Week, the largest sailing regatta in Atlantic Canada. If you haven't experienced sailing and wish to, charters are available out of Deep Cove, 20 km (12.4 mi.) east of Chester (Take Route 3 east and turn right onto Route 329 at East River).

Camping overnight at Graves Island Provincial Park offers beach access and trails on a remote coastal peninsula surrounded on three sides by ocean. To reach the park, travel east from Chester on Route 3 and watch for signs to your right just past East Chester. It's always best to phone ahead to make sure campsites are available (902-275-9917).

Map: Mahone Bay to Chester and Tancook Island   4.4.4

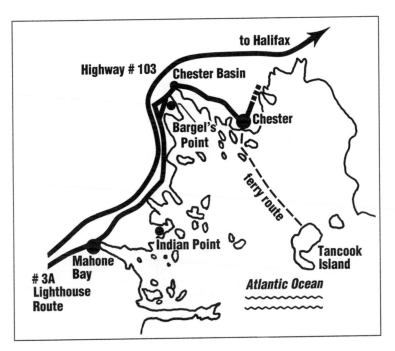

4.4.5 Activities: Queensland Beach
Dive the Waves at Queensland Beach

A day east of Chester, culminating in a rejuvenating dip in the surf at Queensland Beach, begins with a tour of the Aspotogan Peninsula, about 35 km (22 mi.) around. Turn right off Route 3 onto Route 329 at East River. This is a beautiful drive or bicycle ride through fishing communities.

Stop at Bayswater Beach Provincial Park for some barbecued fish on the grill. Pick up some fresh catch at a nearby wharf or store, wrap it in tin foil with onions, tomatoes, and herbs, then bake in the coals for 20 minutes for a fine lunch.

Continue along through Aspotogan and Northwest Cove, Mill Cove, and Fox Point (where there is a lobster pound), then pick up Route 3 again at Hubbards. Further along is Queensland Beach where you can spend the afternoon body surfing and sunning. Other sandy stretches in the vicinity are at Cleveland's Beach and Black Point Beach. Sample some local fish or clams and chips to see how they compare with the clams in Yarmouth, the best around.

4.4.6 Map: Chester to Black Point

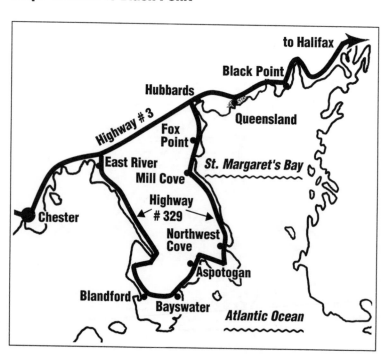

The Atlantic Coast's
South Shore

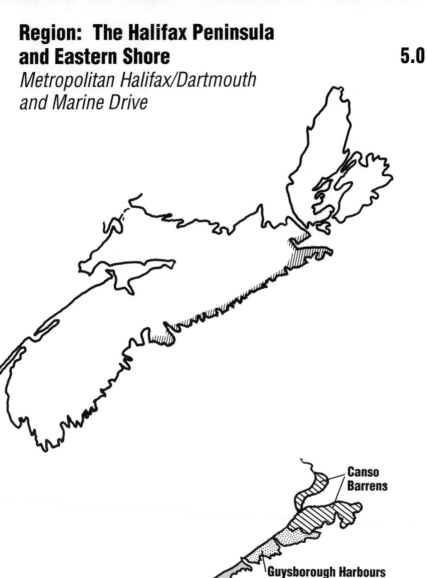

Canso Barrens

Guysborough Harbours

Bay of Islands

Eastern Shore Beaches

Pennant Barrens

Eroded granite headlands and coastal barrens, fine sand beaches, rocky islands, and long, drowned estuaries, are all features of the Eastern Shore.

The region is divided into five areas: Peggy's Cove to Halifax, Lawrencetown Beach to Sheet Harbour, Tangier to Ecum Secum, Liscombe to Tor Bay, and Tor Bay to Canso. The areas are ecologically diverse with granite barrens, beaches and islands, and quartzite headlands all represented. Long considered Nova Scotia's most unexplored region, the Eastern Shore contains important breeding habitat for many birds.

5.1   Area: Peggy's Cove to Halifax — Pennant Barrens

Travelling eastward from Aspotogan on the South Shore's Blandford Peninsula, one enters a landscape of grey flecked boulders, a granite barrens known as the Pennant Barrens. The area includes the promontory between Halifax Harbour and St. Margaret's Bay, beginning at Aspotogan. Across the water is Peggy's Cove, the most photographed granite in the world, modified over time into large blocks to climb and explore.

This granite promontory, elevated above the surrounding upland surface, with its thin rocky tills and exposed bedrock, makes an extensive coastal barrens with bogs. Rare arctic-alpine flora can be found along the rocky shoreline swept clear of sediment.

In this area, the till contains many glacial erratics dumped randomly across the landscape. The sediment supply is very limited and only the accumulations carried inland by the sea provide enough sand for beaches such as Crystal Crescent.

Much of the area is covered by coastal barrens, with lichens, Broom Crowberry, and Reindeer Moss, interspersed with small sphagnum and sedge bogs. Where exposure to wind and spray is most severe, stunted white spruce is usually found. Black spruce, larch, and balsam fir occur on more sheltered sites, with maple and birch.

The shoreline is mainly rocky with low cliffs, some islands and a few sand beaches; it does not provide much suitable habitat for shorebirds or waterfowl. Breeding birds include gulls, Osprey, Great Blue Herons, and there are a few Bald Eagle breeding sites and Double-Crested Cormorant colonies. Productive plankton areas bring whales to feed, particularly in the late summer.

Glacial erratics dot the hills at Peggy's Cove and accessible bogs in the area are wonderful photo opportunities if bog flora such as the Pitcher Plant, Sundew, and Moccasin Flowers are of interest. The Peggy's Cove Conservation Area and adjacent Provincial Park Reserve protect the coastal barrens and bogs. Peggy's Cove has a longstanding fishing tradition captured in the paintings of local artist James DeGarthe, some of which are on view in a local

The erratics at Peggy's Cove conservation area brood over the area's most popular vista.

art studio. He has also carved a sculpture along a 30 m (98 ft) face of a granite outcrop in the village.

From Peggy's Cove, you can travel east to West Dover, an example of a lichen-dominated, virtually treeless barren. Also in the area are the villages of East Dover and Shad Bay. This heavily-wooded drive leads to Prospect, a scenic fishing village facing the open Atlantic. From here, it is a short drive from White's Lake to Terence Bay with a sheltered beach and a memorial to the wreck of the *SS Atlantic* in 1873.

On the Halifax Harbour side of the promontory, a drive along the coast to Purcell's Cove goes past several yacht clubs and wharves from which ocean and harbour charters are available. At York Redoubt National Historic Site there is a fortification begun in the 1790s to serve as a strategic harbour defense. From Herring Cove to Portuguese Cove, you can see examples of granite and meguma sediments joined—loose blocks of country rock "floating" in granite. On this drive you pass Chebucto Head, the actual mouth of Halifax Harbour, from which whales can sometimes be seen feeding in the summer. Here, large white crystals of feldspar showing flow patterns are apparent in the granite.

Duncan's Cove, at Chebucto Head, is a large area of coastal barrens with a number of rare plants. At Sambro, fishing and boat-building are important industries. The lighthouse in this village, dating from 1759, is considered by many to be the oldest lighthouse still in use in North America. The lens used between 1906 and 1967 is on display at the Maritime Museum of the Atlantic in Halifax. Nearby Crystal Crescent Beach is a popular spot for swimming, hiking, and relaxing. There is a coastal hike, 10 km (6 mi.) along a smooth granite rock beach, covered with the debris from shipwrecks, to Pennant Point.

Lighthouses are present at Sambro Island, McNab's Island and Peggy's Cove.

5.1.1   Activities: Peggy's Cove
Walk among Timeless Monuments —
The Granite Erratics of Peggy's Cove

The famous Peggy's Cove lighthouse is symbolic sentinel of man's presence on the rugged coast of Nova Scotia. Perhaps more mysterious a monument is the granite boulder that sits perched near the cove as it was left by glacial retreat 290 million years ago.

To get to this great natural statue, take the Bay Road exit at the Halifax Rotary and follow Route 103 to the Peggy's Cove exit. This Route 333 will take you along the west side of the Halifax Peninsula through some wonderful coastal scenery. Just before the cove, you'll begin to see a strange barren "moonscape" terrain with granite boulders distributed erratically (thus the term "erratics") over the expanse. One large boulder stands out as the largest and most prominently located. You can hike to the top for a closer look at the boulder and a great view of the cove.

After a hike to the boulder, continue on into the cove to climb the rocks and view the seascape from the lighthouse. Look for DeGarthe's granite relief sculpture depicting fishermen whose lives were as hard as the granite he so skillfully sculpted during the last years of his life.

Head back to Halifax along Route 333 east through West Dover and Shad Bay.

Map: Halifax/Peggy's Cove/Tantallon

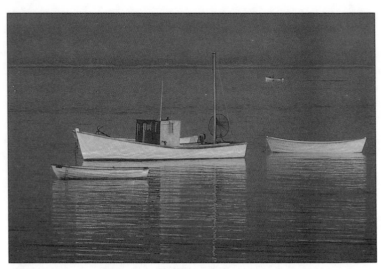

Fishing villages along the coast provide popular cycling routes.

5.1.3   **Activities: Purcell's Cove to Cape Sambro and Back Cycle the Peninsula**

A popular cycling circuit for Haligonians is the Purcell's Cove to Cape Sambro loop, a challenging, approximately 35 km (22 mi.) trip that takes you through fishing communities to Crystal Crescent Beach and back inland. This is a great way to taste salt and test your legs, especially on the Purcell's Cove Hill.

If you don't have your own bike, rentals are available from Freewheeling Bicycle Adventures in Boutilier's Point (902-826-2437). Rentals require a credit card deposit and the bikes can be delivered to you in Halifax and picked up at a prearranged place.

Begin your journey at the Halifax Rotary. Take the exit to Purcell's Cove/ Herring Cove, turn left at the top of the hill at the lights and continue along Route 253 all the way to Herring Cove where you follow Route 349 to Duncan's Cove. A side detour 1 km (.6 mi.) to the left will take you to Chebucto Head coastal barrens. There is a look-off here and its imposing location is a good place to stop for lunch. Backtrack to the highway and continue on through the fishing village of Ketch Harbour to Sambro where you'll see signs to Crystal Crescent Beach. Take a swim in the invigorating surf (not for the easily chilled) and hike along the coastal paths. Continue back to the intersection and take Route 349 inland to Harrietsfield and Spryfield where a glorious downhill run will bring you back to your point of departure.

Map: Purcell's Cove to Sambro   5.1.4

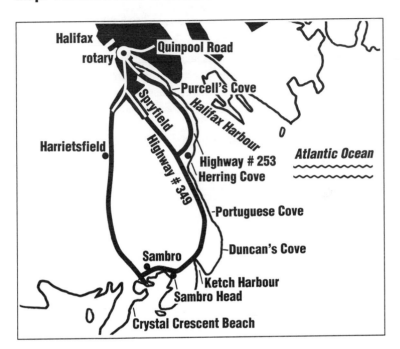

Halifax rotary
Quinpool Road
Purcell's Cove
Halifax Harbour
Spryfield
Highway # 349
Harrietsfield
Highway # 253
Herring Cove
Atlantic Ocean
Portuguese Cove
Duncan's Cove
Sambro
Ketch Harbour
Sambro Head
Crystal Crescent Beach

Activities: Purcell's Cove   5.1.5
Charter a Cape Islander and Jig for Cod

Leave the granite shores of Halifax Harbour and head southeast toward the Atlantic Ocean. Halifax's fortifications were so well-placed that it was never attacked. York Redoubt, now a national park, was the site of a manned fort in the 1700s and again during World Wars I and II. MacNab's Fort, George's Island, and Point Pleasant Park were also armed to protect the harbour.

There is a family-run boat charter at 553 Purcell's Cove Road (902-479-2900). They'll fillet your fish and prepare you chowder on request. A relaxed atmosphere, personalized service and jigging for fish are offered. Some of the other charters provide more fishing methods such as drift fishing and trolling (902-422-3608). Others specialize in shark and sword fishing (902-477-9630). The tourist centre in Halifax can provide you with more detail on the types of charters available.

An afternoon at sea can give you the chance to jig for cod and other bottom fish, watch for whales and porpoises, stop for a picnic on McNab's Island, eat chowder, mussels and lobster on board and have an "ugliest sculpin contest."

The Halifax Peninsula and Eastern Shore

Sculpins are the horny-winged, bright red fish, "a cross between a dragon and a cod" that love to frustrate the fishermen.

Charters are available in Purcell's Cove (Take Purcell's Cove exit, left at Herring Cove lights. Go approximately 7 km (4.3 mi.) to the main cove dock. You can also charter boats from the Halifax waterfront (foot of Duke and Lower Water Streets), and the Dartmouth waterfront. Take warm clothes no matter what the weather on land, sun block, hat, sunglasses, food, and beverages (a thermos of hot tea or chocolate is nice), and a camera.

5.2   Area: Lawrencetown Beach to Sheet Harbour — Eastern Shore Beaches

Drowned by the sea, long inlets at Chezzetcook, Petpeswick, Musquodoboit, and Jeddore deeply indent the coast from Halifax, eastward to Owl's Head near Clam Harbour. Reworked by the sea, ample coastal sediment builds spits and barrier beaches between headlands and islands. Along this protective coast, birds rest during their migratory flights and sometimes overwinter.

Most inlets are drowned river estuaries, the salt water flooding diminutive freshwater runs. The bedrock is greywacke, with bands of slate, folded parallel to the coastline. Loose cobble quartzite till forms the glacial deposits and is overlain in the Chezzetcook to Lawrencetown and Clam Bay areas with red-brown drumlin tills. The irregularity characteristic of a youthful submergant coastline is being smoothed off here as sediment is redistributed. Sand and gravel are supplied from the erosion of deep glacial materials and outwash deposits along the coast. Spits and barrier beaches connecting promontories and islands protect the large, shallow estuaries from ocean waves, allowing salt marshes to develop.

The coastal white spruce, balsam fir forest with maple and birch predominates. On old farm lands and drumlins, pure stands of white spruce are common. Salt marsh and sand dune plant communities, and large beds of eelgrass, which provide food for Canada Geese and Black Duck, are common.

This is an area similar to the LaHave Drumlin district on the South Shore, where sheltered inlets favour southerly marine fauna and exposed rocky shores support northerly species. Warmer water brings in warm water fish and invertebrates in the summer. Recently, sea urchins have devastated the marine algae population, but this trend is reversing with a rapid seaweed recovery underway.

Cole Harbour, Chezzetcook Inlet, Petpeswick Inlet, and Musquodoboit Harbour are important habitats for significant numbers of waterfowl. In spring, and again in October, the largest numbers of Canada Geese and Black Duck in Nova Scotia stop over. Black Ducks breed in coastal barrier beach, estuary,

The Halifax Peninsula and Eastern Shore

and coastal marsh habitat. Other overwintering bird are the Common Goldeneye and, occasionally, Scaup. Piping Plovers nest at Lawrencetown and Clam Bay. Scattered nesting habitat for Bald Eagles is also found here.

At Cole Harbour, the Cole Harbour Heritage Farm Museum, records the area's links with the sea and the Halifax market. The Cole Harbour Dyke area is a favourite resting area for migrating Canada Geese and various sea birds in spring and fall.

Lawrencetown has a supervised beach but be forewarned; the undertow is extremely dangerous and even strong swimmers have perished here. There is an extensive salt marsh at West Lawrencetown.

At Three Fathom Harbour, the elongated Porter's Lake system is connected by a canal to the Atlantic. A Marina Park with launching facilities is located at the Porters Lake Bridge.

Continue along the coast through Seaforth, Grand Desert to West Chezzetcook, settled by French Acadians.

Musquodoboit Harbour is the largest community along the western portion of the Eastern Shore. Fishing, forestry, and light manufacturing are the principal industries. The Musquodoboit Railway Museum contains many artifacts, photographs and maps, illustrating the importance the railway once was to this small town.

Beautiful Martinique Beach lies near Petpeswick Harbour on the inlet of the same name. The longest beach in Nova Scotia at 4.8 km (3 mi.), it offers a day-use park with supervised swimming. Behind the beach is a game sanctuary that teems with birds in the fall and winter months. On the other side of the harbour is Pleasant Point, the Nova Scotia Department of Fisheries shellfish hatchery where visitors are welcome. A lighthouse stands at the end of the Kent Road.

Fisherman's Life Museum, the original home of a turn-of-the-century fisherman, James Myers Jr., who had thirteen daughters, has been completely restored to its original state and amply recaptures the simple surroundings this family occupied while making their living from the sea.

Clam Harbour has an extensive beach of hard white sand and fine surf bathing. The beach is being developed as part of the Eastern Shore Seaside Park System and features a lifeguard tower, hiking trail, and picnic area. The annual Clam Harbour Beach Sand Sculpting Contest is held in mid-August.

Owls Head Harbour is a picturesque community that overlooks the indented coastline.

Conrads Island, part of the Cole Harbour–Lawrencetown Coastal Heritage Provincial Park System has fine examples of various coastal habitats and processes, including sand dunes and cobble beaches. It is an excellent place for birding.

The Halifax Peninsula and Eastern Shore

5.2.1   Activities: Lawrencetown Beach
Wind Surf at Lawrencetown Beach

Tales are told of brave rescues at Lawrencetown Beach, the nearest sand beach east of Halifax. A strong undertow at the west end of the beach requires caution. Since the sport of windsurfing has become popular in the last decade, a new breed of amphibious human can be seen riding the surf.

Lawrencetown Beach is located on Route 207 along the Eastern Shore. To get there from Halifax, cross the Angus L. MacDonald bridge into Dartmouth, turn right onto Wyse Road and left at Octerloney to Prince Albert Road and Route 7. At the rotary, take the exit to Cole Harbour (Route 207) and travel through strip mall sprawl and traffic lights until you're over a hill and out of the city. Continue on until the ocean appears. There are no windsurfing rentals here so this activity is not for the novice, but judging by the number of fluorescent-clad surfers and sails, this is a popular destination for the master and journeyman enthusiast.

Continue along Route 207 and turn left onto Route 7 to Porter's Lake, a provincial campground, where warmer lake water will soothe strained muscles and wash away the salt.

5.2.2   Map: Dartmouth to Lawrencetown Beach

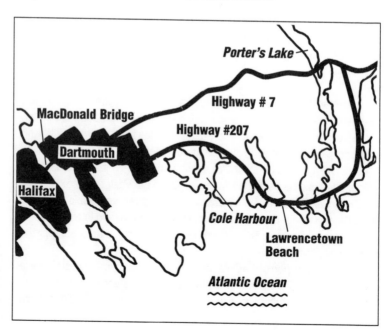

Activities: Meagher's Grant
Canoe Nearby Rivers Musquodoboit, Shubenacadie, and Stewiacke

There are three rivers in this area which flow into the Atlantic: the Musquodoboit, Shubenacadie, and the Stewiacke. Between them, they comprise 180 km (112 mi.) of paddling.

Canoeing on these rivers can be either a day outing or an extended adventure. Canoe rentals at Meagher's Grant, about 35km (22 mi.) inland from Musquodoboit Harbour (turn left toward Middle Musquodoboit) make this activity accessible to those without equipment. They also have a shuttle service to points along the Musquodoboit River. Overnight parking is available if you wish to camp overnight on the river. Ask for directions for the canoe rentals at E.K. Parker's General Store in Meagher's Grant.

The owners of the canoe rental will be able to tell you about canoeing the Shubenacadie and Stewiacke Rivers, two very lovely rivers located within one-half hour's drive. Canoe waterways maps printed on a scale of 1:15,840 provide the most detailed information available on Stewiacke, Musquodoboit (2 maps), and Shubenacadie (2 maps) Rivers. These are available from Land Registration and Information Service, Amherst (902-667-7231), N.S. Government Bookstore, Halifax (902-424-7580) and The Trail Shop, Halifax (902-423-8736).

Fly fishing on the Stewiacke River.

The Halifax Peninsula and Eastern Shore

5.2.4   Map: Musquodoboit/Shubenacadie/Stewiacke Rivers

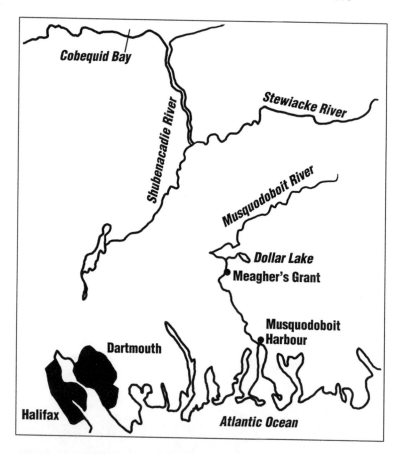

5.2.5   Activities: Martinique and Clam Harbour
Being at Beaches

Five kilometres (3 mi.) of fine sand make Martinique Beach a jogger's or a walker's paradise. To get there, head east from Lawrencetown Beach until Route 207 connects with Route 7 at the Head of Chezzetcook. Turn right and continue to Musquodoboit Harbour where you take a right along a long, winding coastal road to Martinique Beach, where shorebirds and waterfowl can be easily spotted.

You will find the water cool but the sun and the sand warm. Swimmers are warned of a dangerous undertow in the cove at the west end of the beach. The grass growing in the sand is called Marram Grass. Its net-like roots have created the beach by trapping sand that wind and water have piled here. The grass may appear sharp and tough but it is, in fact, very fragile. Too much foot traffic or driving vehicles over the dunes can kill this vital dune cover, resulting in "blowouts," places where the sand has been removed by wind. You are strongly advised to help protect the beach by not walking on the Marram Grass.

The Martinique area also contains a waterfowl sanctuary which is accessible by obtaining a permit from the Musquodoboit office of the Department of Lands and Forests.

Clam Harbour Beach is a beautiful place where dogwood, wild strawberry, and iris bloom against an eroded greywacke and slate bedrock backdrop. Continuing east from Halifax, Clam Harbour Beach is about 4 km (2.5 mi.) east of Clam Bay. A sign indicating Clam Harbour Provincial Picnic Park is on your right. This road leads you to one of Nova Scotia's most, if not *the* most, outstanding beaches.

After sunning and swimming in the surf, take the 4 km (2.5 mi.) hike up the beach to a chain of tiny private beaches where the clear Eastern Shore waters are ideal for snorkelling. The path meanders up and down over creviced, lichen and club moss-covered cliffs. Here beach plants such as beach pea, violet, and iris mingle with the moss clumps greening the rocks.

Map: Lawrencetown Beach to Ship Harbour   5.2.6

The Halifax Peninsula and Eastern Shore

5.2.7 **Activities: Jeddore Oyster Ponds**
Tour the Fisherman's Life Museum

In Jeddore Oyster Ponds, a nineteenth century fisherman's home has been preserved as a museum. It is one of the Nova Scotia Museum's chain of historic houses that have been preserved and restored to give us a glimpse of the past.

The home in Jeddore Oyster Ponds is a typical inshore fisherman's house of the early 1900s. Built in 1857 by James Myers and remodelled several times, this small house was later home to his youngest son's family of thirteen. The house has been refurbished with the ordinary things of rural living from Nova Scotian communities: a parlour pump organ, hooked mats, grandmother's favourite dishes, and a wood stove.

To find the Fisherman's Life Museum, continue east along Route 7 from Musquodoboit Harbour and, after crossing the Salmon River Bridge, look for a sign announcing the museum.

After spending an hour or so at the museum, take a walk up the road to the seafood restaurant and sample steamed blue mussels, the treasure of the Eastern Shore's growing aquaculture industry. An interpretive centre about aquaculture in the area has been built and is open regular hours. Ask your friendly Nova Scotian hosts for directions to the centre.

Lawrencetown is famous for sunning, swimming, and for challenging surfing.

The Halifax Peninsula
and Eastern Shore

Map: Jeddore Oyster Ponds   5.2.8

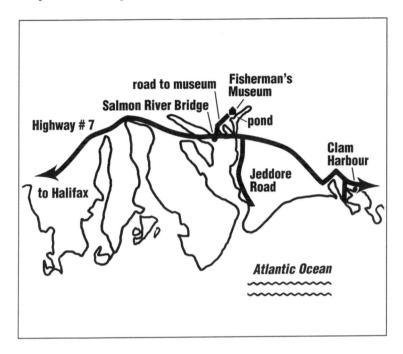

Area: Tangier to Ecum Secum — Bay of Islands   5.3

Extending from the headlands of Little Harbour (southwest of Ship Harbour) to
Liscomb Harbour and north to the head of major inlets, is an area of submerged
rocky coastline with a parallel structure of elongated offshore islands. Variable
sediment produces a variety of coastal habitats from rocky shore with extensive
seaweed, to salt marsh.

Here, offshore islands have formed as the low, eroded headlands were
drowned during recent coastal submergence. They have an average elevation
of less than 15 m (50 ft) and are divided into groups by bays and inlets. Drumlin,
which occur in scatted groups forming headlands all along the Eastern Shore,
are rarely found as islands in this area.

The coastal white spruce-balsam fir forest predominates here as well with
some maple and birch mixed in on less exposed sites. On the wetter soils, black
spruce, larch and balsam fir are found. Lonely Barrens cover many of the
headlands, and stunted trees appear stubbornly to break the flat expanse. A
regular pattern of a ridge of white spruce and depressions of small bogs and
black spruce weaves its way along the coast. Many of the islands offshore have

The Halifax Peninsula
and Eastern Shore

been deforested by the combined effects of exposure and cormorant guano and may not regain a tree cover.

This is a land of low-lying rocky shores with small beach and salt marsh areas. Lack of sediment produces masses of seaweed especially along the rocky quartzite shoals which stretch out into the water.

Together with the Guysborough Harbours district, the Bay of Islands forms a major portion of the Common Eider breeding habitat for Nova Scotia. As well as the significant breeding habitat on the islands, considerable numbers of waterfowl migrate through in spring and fall including scoters, Black Duck, Oldsquaw, and Canada Geese. Some Oldsquaw, Black Duck, and Common Goldeneye remain during the winter. Seals are common on the islands and rocky shoals.

You will notice thousands of white buoys in the water at Ship Harbour. This is North America's largest cultivated mussel farm. The road follows the eastern shore of the harbour through East Ship Harbour and then through Murphy Cove and Pleasant Harbour.

Tangier is the site of one of Nova Scotia's earliest gold mines. Opened in 1860, it prospered for 30 years. It is claimed that the best smoked salmon in the world is made right here by Willy Krauch. A rare chance for coastal canoeing is also offered to the experienced and novice alike.

At Moose River Gold Mines, a provincial park and community museum commemorates the mining disaster in 1936 where three men were trapped at the 43 m (141 ft) level for 10 days. This was the first disaster in North America to be covered by continuous, on-the-spot radio news broadcasts heard by 100 million listeners.

Spry Harbour is a typical Eastern Shore fishing village. Nearby is Taylor's Head Provincial Park, which features a sandy beach, a walking trail, sand volcanoes and slump structures, the formation of a landslide that develops where strong, resistant rocks overlie weak rocks.

Spry Bay features excellent views of Tomlee Bay and Mushaboom Harbour and has an ancient Micmac burial ground.

The name Mushaboom comes from a Micmac word meaning "hair of the dead lying there" based on the belief that small people or fairies used to play there, seizing each other by the locks, pulling out handfuls of hair, and leaving them lying on the ground.

Sheet Harbour was settled in 1784 by refugees and veterans of the American Revolution and became a prosperous centre for the lumbering industry. Today, an annual Seaside Festival is held here.

At Beaver Harbour, a Micmac legend describes Glooscap throwing one of the large shoreline rocks at his friend beaver.

Port Dufferin was named in honour of the Marquis of Dufferin, Governor

General of Canada. Considerable quantities of gold have been mined in this area. East of Dufferin, the road passes through the coastal villages of East Quoddy, Harrigan Cove, and Moosehead.

At nearby Moser River, a sign indicates a road to a Department of Lands and Forests' fish-raising station at Kelly Lake.

The road leads back to the coast at Necum Teuch and into Ecum Secum and Marie Joseph. Two pleasant picnic sites are located in the area: Juds Pool on the Ecum Secum River, and just west of Marie Joseph, a site overlooking the ocean.

Activities: Tangier   5.3.1
Enrol in a Sea Kayak Clinic

Though most famous for Willy Krauch's smoked salmon (served to royalty and VIPs around the world), Tangier is also becoming known as the provincial centre for ocean or sea kayaking. If you think you've seen Nova Scotia by travelling its roads on bicycle or on foot, Scott Cunningham, the resident sea kayak guru says, "You ain't seen nothin' yet!"

Nova Scotia's 7,000 km (4,350 mi.) of coastline provides a lot of paddling and visual treats beyond imagination. Add to this thousands of offshore islands and you have your summer vacations laid out for years to come. And almost all this coastline can be explored in relative solitude because natives and visitors alike use only small sections of the shoreline. You will seldom encounter fishing or pleasure craft, and even less frequently other paddlers.

To begin, find the sea kayak outfitter, Scott Cunningham, a knowledgeable naturalist and kayaker, on Mason's Point Road in Tangier (there's a sign to your right) (902-772-2774). Here you can take part in a day-long clinic where you'll learn how to choose a boat, the basic paddling strokes, and the fundamentals of sea kayak touring. In the afternoon, you'll visit the nearby, uninhabited offshore islands in search of seals and seabirds. All equipment is supplied and no prior experience is needed. "Just showing up is enough!" Cunningham says. You can find out more from any tourist information centre.

The Halifax Peninsula and Eastern Shore

Nova Scotia's 7,000 kilometres of coastline provides exciting visual treats for kayakers.

Map: East Ship Harbour to Tangier

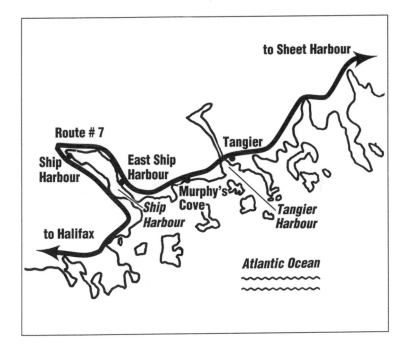

Activities: Tangier
See the Islands of Birds by Kayak

Off the coast of Tangier are hundreds of islands with names like "The Pancake," "Pumpkin," and "Brokenback," describing their shape or other distinguishing features. These islands are inhabited exclusively by birds and seals.

To mark their importance as nesting habitat for at least 12 species of sea birds, the Wildlife Division of the Nova Scotia Department of Lands and Forests proclaimed this region as the "Eastern Shore Island Management Area."

The area is comprised of approximately 50 vegetated islands and islets and 10 non-vegetated islets or ledges formed when low, eroded headlands were drowned during recent coastal submergence. They are notable as nesting colonies for the Black Guillemot, Common Eider, Great Blue Heron, Osprey, Double-Crested Cormorant, Leach's Storm Petrel, Great Black Back and Herring Gull and Arctic, Common and Roseate Terns.

The few people who visit these islands are either biologists, bird-watchers, fishermen, or the latest breed of island hopper—the sea kayaker. In July, the

The Halifax Peninsula and Eastern Shore

125

height of the nesting season, the local sea kayaking outfitter takes 3, 5 and 7-day excursions to this area. You will have a chance to observe Herring and Black Back Gulls, terns, guillemots, Eider Ducks, petrels, and Osprey in various stages of development.

It is a saltwater paddler's paradise! Uninhabited and isolated, these islands provide a journey of exploration with something new and unexpected around each corner: rocky headlands and sand spits, beaches and turquoise lagoons, dense spruce and barren bedrock with glacial erratics poised in strange positions. The geology has been laid bare by the relentless attack of the ocean. Seals and seabird colonies reflect an environment novel to one who has spent his or her paddling days on interior waters.

5.4   Area: Liscomb to Tor Bay — Guysborough Harbours

This area extends from Marie Joseph to New Harbour Cove and exists along the Chedabucto Fault Line. Slip movements have caused a series of parallel faults to develop, dividing the bedrock into a number of blocks. Weaknesses in the fault pattern have been exploited by rivers producing relatively straight valleys. These have been inundated by the sea so that they form very long, narrow inlets. Sheet Harbour, Indian Harbour, Country Harbour, Isaac's Harbour, and New Harbour are all examples of these drowned, fault controlled river valleys. They tend to be narrow and steep-sided providing interesting variety in an otherwise uniform terrain.

Liscomb Harbour and Fishermans Harbour (near Port Bickerton) have been formed by erosion of the relatively weak slate bedrock. The east-west orientation of these two harbours contrasts with the northwest-southeast orientation of all other harbours. The only comparable feature on the Atlantic Coast region is Yarmouth Sound.

A single group of drumlins made up of red-brown till from the Carboniferous strata to the north crosses the area parallel to Indian Harbour River. The drumlins reach the coast between Holland Harbour and St. Marys Bay where they form coastal bluffs. Thick sand and gravel deposits choke the valleys and impede drainage. New Harbour Lake is impounded by a gravel barrier across the valley at Port Hillford.

The coastal sediment is limited and there are few sand beaches. Coastal fringe deposits tend to be rocky or cobble. On better drained soils the forest is mixed, but predominantly softwoods—white spruce, balsam fir with maple and birch. On the wetter soils the main species are black spruce, larch and balsam fir. Huckleberry brush is common on the barren and semi-barren areas, which are extensive.

Little salt marsh occurs along this coast, as so little sediment is available, but there are some eelgrass beds.

Because the snowfall is considerably less than elsewhere on the coast, this area forms an important wintering area for deer. This area is also an important breeding and feeding habitat for waterfowl, both resident and migratory, and along with the Bay of Islands, constitutes a major portion of the breeding and brood-raising habitat for the Common Eider in Nova Scotia.

Between Liscomb Mills and Liscomb is Spanish Ship Bay. In these sheltered coves, mussels, European oysters, trout, and salmon are grown. Deep-sea fishing is also good here. The area around Liscomb is one of the most scenic parts of the Eastern Shore.

Much of this coastal area is inaccessible by highway as the main road travels inland from Spanish Ship Bay to Melrose. From here you can proceed to Isaacs Harbour North via the Country Harbour ferry, a seven-minute ride. A delightful view up the length of Country Harbour awaits you as you drive down the hill to the ferry terminus at Port Bickerton, a fishing community supported by a seafood-processing plant.

Isaac's Harbour, near Isaac's Harbour North, leads through Goldboro, Drumhead, Seal Harbour, Coddle Harbour, and New Harbour, which has a sandy beach. There are foxberry and cranberry barrens in this area.

At Tor Bay there is a provincial picnic park on an ocean beach. A plaque commemorates the landing at Tor Bay in 1875 of the first commercial cable to successfully transmit messages from England to mainland North America.

Activities: Liscomb Mills   5.4.1
Do it All (Fish, Canoe, Cruise, Swim) at Liscomb Lodge

You can pack in several coastal adventures under the umbrella of summer lodge living: cottages, chalets, lodge rooms, and a dining room serving traditional meals. Hike the trails near the lodge or arrange a long hike to Sherbrooke Village 25 km (15.5 mi.) away, a living museum which takes you back to the mid 1800s when Sherbrooke was a major lumbering and ship building centre. Have someone drive you back to the lodge and relax with a plate of steamed mussels, smoked salmon, or Eastern Shore lobster, considered the best in the province.

Liscomb is a fisherman's haven, situated in one of Nova Scotia's vestiges of excellent inland angling. A marina provides canoe rentals and deep sea fishing charters.

To get to Liscomb, continue along Route 7, east from Sheet Harbour. It's a long winding road which follows the coast. Although the human population declines as you proceed, you are heading into bird country as the islands

The Halifax Peninsula and Eastern Shore

offshore are incubators for sea birds and waterfowl of many species. Keep your eyes open for three large birds in particular: Great Blue Herons standing motionless in salt marsh or beach terrain; Osprey flying overhead; and the silent coal black Double-Crested Cormorant.

The heron nests are crudely constructed structures high among the topmost branches of tall trees; the Osprey's nest is similar but may be found on rocky cliffs and telephone poles and very rarely on the ground; cormorants nest atop rocks, cliffs, and in tree tops.

If you take a boat charter, you may well see a variety of sea birds flying or bobbing, the most common of which are the gulls, their numbers growing, due to their penchant for eating human garbage.

Whether you stay in Liscomb a day or a week, there's much to do and see.

The barrens provide a breeding ground for a wide variety of bird life.

Map: Liscomb Mills

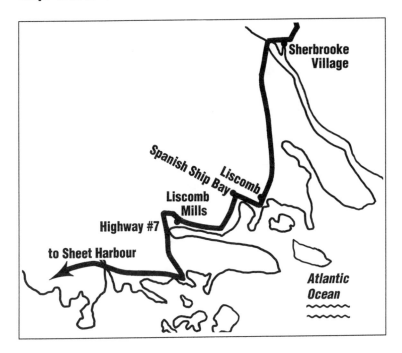

Activities: Tor Bay
Walk the Barrens

Most of us who live among trees take them for granted. Nova Scotia, however, is not fully treed and its Eastern Shore is a fine example of barren habitat.

If you travel the long road (Routes 211 and 316) to the easterly end of mainland Nova Scotia at Cape Canso, and ultimately to the entrance to Cape Breton Island, you will find a land dominated by granite which forms headlands and knolls elevated well above the adjacent land. Here you leave the sediment-plentiful land of beaches and drumlins and enter the coastal barrens, a quite strange and alien landscape. Granite boulders (erratics) left by retreating glaciers appear like extraterrestrials and trees only occur in gnarled forms. Vegetation includes Sheep Laurel, Huckleberry brush, Labrador Tea, scrubby black spruce, bracken and alders.

The barrens do not provide productive habitat for many animal species, but the rocky southeastern coast is a breeding ground for gulls, cormorants, herons, terns, and the Common Eider.

To learn about the coastal environment of this part of Nova Scotia, make

The Halifax Peninsula
and Eastern Shore

your destination Tor Bay Provincial Park where an interpretive display describes
the life of the coastal barrens. Access to a sand beach, dunes, and salt marsh
is also provided.

Enjoying the sandy sweep of Taylor's Head Beach.

5.4.4   Map: Tor Bay to Grassy Island

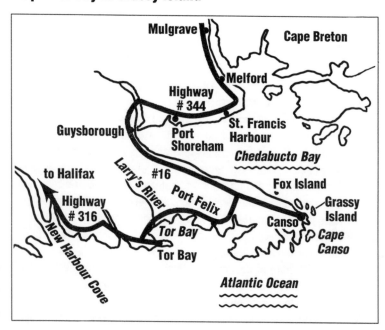

Area: Tor Bay to Canso — Canso Barrens   5.5

The straight northern coastline is a sharp contrast to the indented south-eastern coast characterized by bays and bedrock islands. Here, extensive areas of exposed rock suggest an inhospitable moonscape. Like its western counterpart at Pennant, the Canso Barrens are dominated by granite where rounded knolls rise to heights of up to 200 m (650 ft) above sea level.

While there is enough soil for a few hardy trees to become established, they are mostly black spruce and balsam fir in dense stands, interspersed with white spruce, maple and birch. In wetter areas, black spruce and larch predominate. The presence of jack pine indicates that extensive fires once raged on the Canso peninsula.

The cold water shore is home to an arctic indicator species, *Mysis gaspensis,* a small shrimp crustacean.

Larry's River was first settled in 1791 by Acadian French from Chezzetcook and was named after Larry Keating, a Halifax man who spent a winter hunting moose in the local woods.

After Larry's River, the road continues through remote coastal areas, twisting around inlets and providing sweeping views of the ocean from higher ground. Port Felix has a fine view of the bay and islands from Chapel Hill.

Founded in 1605, Canso is situated at the entrance to Chedabucto Bay and is sheltered from the ocean by Grassy Island. The name comes from the Micmac word, *Kamsok,* meaning "opposite the lofty cliffs."

Canso was an important French fishing station in the seventeenth century, but after 1720, a small British garrison was stationed here and fortifications were constructed on Grassy Island to protect the community from the French at Louisbourg. No sign of the historic fort remains, but the public may visit the island which is a new National Historic Site.

The office of the Western Union transatlantic cable company opened in Canso in 1881. Many of the original company houses are still occupied and may be seen overlooking the Atlantic. The first cables came ashore at Canso in July 1884.

The Seamen's Memorial is framed by the ribs of a boat. It is dedicated to all those local residents lost at sea and commemorates the close connections of the Canso area with the Atlantic Ocean. The Canso Museum in the Whitman House is also worth a visit.

Guysborough, known first as Chedabucto, meaning "the great long harbour," was the site of a fishing station established by Nicholas Denys in the 1650s and later fortified by the French. A few English settlers pioneered in the 1760s, and the Loyalists arrived in the area after 1784. The Nova Scotia Department of Lands and Forests operates Boylston Provincial Park (located between

The Halifax Peninsula and Eastern Shore

131

Guysborough and Milford Station) which has camping and picnic facilities.

Boylston was settled in 1786 by New England Loyalists. From here, the road follows Cape Argos, partially hugging the coast and passing through wooded areas with occasional pockets of farmland. Port Shoreham was settled by Loyalists in 1786. From St. Francis Harbour, Eddy Point Light is visible.

One of the finest harbours in the world is located at Mulgrave.

5.5.1   Activities: Canso
Of Fish Stations and Fortifications
Explore Grassy Island National Park

At the easternmost tip of mainland Nova Scotia lies Canso, a fishing centre for over 400 years. Here you can take a trip to Grassy Island, the newest National Historic Park, still under development, as well as visit the Grassy Island Interpretive Centre on Main Street in Canso. The history of Canso and Grassy Island is long and fascinating.

As early as the 16th century, French, Basque, and Portuguese fishermen frequented the waters off Canso in pursuit of the abundant cod. By the late 17th century, French and New England fishermen coexisted peaceably on the Canso Islands despite the rivalry between their governments.

In 1713, Britain claimed ownership of the Canso Islands by the terms of the treaty of Utrecht. France disputed this claim, but gradually the French fishery shifted to the fortress town of Louisbourg.

The Canso fishery developed hard on the heels of the invention of the New England schooner. These decked vessels were larger, faster, and more versatile than the French *chaloupes*.

The New England fishery at Grassy Island was seasonal. Each spring, schooner crews would set out from New England, primarily Massachusetts, and make for Canso. It was not uncommon for over 200 vessels to put into Canso in a single season. Each crew of five or six men fished 50-90 miles offshore, then landed their catch to be split, gutted, and dried on shore.

Once dried, the fish were carried to European and West Indian markets aboard sack ships (transport vessels). The fishermen returned to New England around late September. In the period 1721-42, the average season's catch came to some 30,000 quintals (over 3,000,000 pounds) of fish.

From the mid-18th century until well into the twentieth, local and New England fishermen continued to land and cure their fish on the Canso Islands. The Canso Islands fishery finally disappeared as fresh fish triumphed over salt cod.

In 1720, Governor Richard Philipps established a garrison on Grassy

Island to assert the British claim under Utrecht. This followed a New England raid on French fishermen in the area in 1718, and a French reprisal during the summer of 1720.

The fort, built with the assistance of New England fishermen, was badly placed near the west end of the island, where portions of it tended to be flooded during high tide. In 1735, Edward How, a merchant, financed construction of a blockhouse on the hill at Grassy Island. The lower fort continued to be used for defensive purposes, but the garrison was housed in the blockhouse and in other buildings on the hill.

In 1744, during the War of the Austrian Succession, a French force from Louisbourg attacked Canso and destroyed all the buildings on Grassy Island. The following year New England forces under William Pepperrell selected Canso as a rendezvous for their attack on Louisbourg. While on the island, the New Englanders erected a new blockhouse and barrack.

Following the successful attack on Louisbourg, Pepperrell withdrew the small garrison he had left on Grassy Island. After the founding of Halifax in 1749, Canso never regained its strategic importance, and the fortifications drifted into ruin.

Today, the island, under the protection of Parks Canada, remains a treeless, windswept memorial to the thriving fishery that contributed so much to the prosperity of 18th-century New England.

Experience 18th-century life at historic Louisbourg.

The Halifax Peninsula and Eastern Shore

Rock climbing and cycling, just two of the many great activities for the outdoor adventurer in Nova Scotia.

Proposed Ecological Sites

The provincial government has designated the following sites "Proposed Ecological Sites." This designation will eventually result in the sites being declared "Fully Protected Ecological Sites" as has been done with Brier Island.

Bay of Fundy and Approaches

Cape St. Mary: Salt marsh and sand dune system of over 300 acres.

Grosses Coques: Salt marsh system.

Brier Island: Two bogs with relict and rare plants, stop-over area for migrating birds and wintering area for common eider.

Ventral Bog: Sphagnum bog with circum-neutral humus layer, presence of disjunct plants, especially skunk cabbage, and possible refugia for coastal plain flora.

Kentville Ravine: Old growth hemlock stand and river flood plain, with rich herbaceous flora.

Cape Split: Primarily deciduous woodlands with rich herbaceous flora. Rare minerals and semiprecious minerals found in amygdaloidal basalt.

Cape d'Or: Wind-swept headland providing arctic-alpine habitat. Notable plants include *Oxytropis johannensis* and *Astragalus robbinsii*.

Moose River: Mature red spruce forest.

Shulie River: Red spruce stand.

Chignecto River: Pure stand of red pine.

The Atlantic Coast's South Shore

Spinney's Heath: Large, undisturbed bog near Central Argyle.

Chebogue Lake: Large inland salt lake with rich beds of eelgrass, also known as Melbourne Lake, is a provincial sanctuary for waterfowl.

Moses Lake: Old growth deciduous forest.

Carter's Beach at South West Port Mouton: Illustrates a classic sand dune successional sequence and has the highest dunes in the Atlantic Coast Region of Nova Scotia. *Sagima nodosa*, Pearlwort is found in the depressions.

Sandhills Beach in Barrington Bay: Combines a sand dune with a *Spartina/Fucus* salt marsh community.

The Halifax Peninsula and Eastern Shore

Bear Cove: An example of a small coastal bog.

Duncan's Cove: A large area of coastal barrens with a number of rare plants.

West Dover: An example of a lichen-dominated, virtually treeless barren.

Conrads Beach: Barrier and dunes.

Little White Island: Dense nesting colonies of cormorants and Common Eider Ducks.

Brokenback Island: One of the few breeding sites for the Fox Sparrow in Nova Scotia, also Osprey nests.

Pumpkin Island: Important nesting site for Leach's Storm Petrel and Black Guillemot.

Horse Island: One of the few islands in the local area which has not been deforested by cormorant nesting.

Bickerton Island: Typical coastal island nesting area for many species.

Tobacco Island: One of few known nesting areas for Fox Sparrow.

Glossary

Alluvial deposits   Material deposited by a river, usually sand gravel.

Amygdaloidal   A rock containing gas bubbles trapped in lava which were subsequently filled with minerals, often semiprecious.

Arctic-alpine   Plants which would more typically occur at a more northerly location or at a higher elevation.

Brackish   Having a salty or briny flavour.

Carboniferous   A period extending from 370 to 270 million years ago.

Crustacean   An invertebrate animal with at least five pairs of jointed legs, such as lobsters, copepods, amphipods, and crabs.

Drowned estuary   An estuary which has become submerged under the sea by geological processes.

Drumlin   A smooth hill formed from deposits of glacial till, whose long axis parallels the direction of flow of the former glacier.

Erosion   The wearing away and removal of material on the earth's surface by forces such as running water, wave action, moving ice, or winds.

Erratic   A large rock or boulder which has been transported some distance from its source, usually by glacial action.

Esker   Long winding ridges of sand and gravel which originated within or beneath glacial ice.

Fault   A fracture or zone of fractures in the earth's crust along which movement has taken place.

Fossils   Any evidence preserved in rock of a once living organism.

Glaciofluvial   Relating to streams fed by melting glaciers, or to the landforms produced by such streams.

Habitat   The natural home or environment of a plant or animal.

Herbaceous   Descriptive of non-woody plants with no above-ground persistent parts.

Glossary

IBP Proposed ecological site A reserve proposed by the Canadian Committee for the International Biological Program. An ecological reserve is a legally protected natural area where human influence is kept to a minimum. Its purpose is to preserve characteristic or regionally rare ecosystems.

Intertidal zone The area between low and high tide marks. It is alternatively covered by water and exposed to the air during each tidal cycle.

Invertebrate An animal which lacks a backbone.

Jurassic The period in geological history between 210 and 140 million years ago.

Molluscs The group of unsegmented invertebrate animals which possess an external or vestigial calcium carbonate shell. It includes clams, snails, and squid.

Moraine Material deposited by a glacier, which has constructional topography independent of the surface on which the material lies.

Old field Abandoned farm land.

Outcrop The area at which a particular rock unit is exposed at the surface.

Outwash deposit A deposit of material laid down by streams flowing away from the front of a glacier.

Phytoplankton Plants of sea or lake which float or drift almost passively. Most are microscopic.

Raised beach A wave-cut platform which is now raised above the present sea level.

Sandstone A sedimentary rock composed predominantly of sand-sized quartz grains.

Terrane A rock formation or series of formations

Transition zone An area linking two series of sediments formed in contrasting environments.

Triassic The geological time period between 247 and 212 million years ago.

Zooplankton The animal component of those organisms drifting or weakly swimming in the ocean, largely at the mercy of prevailing currents.